"Engaging the Enemy"

Demons & Deliverance

The Personal Study Notes of

Dr. Ray A. Freeman

Ray Freeman Ministries
604 Ridge Rd.
Kokomo, IN. 46901
U.S.A.

Demons & Deliverance

This book is produced for those who want an understanding of the powers that we, as Christians, are working against.

It is my prayer that God will cause this study to strengthen you in your faith and give an understanding of what we have as BELIEVERS.

Ray Freeman Ministries
604 Ridge Rd.
Kokomo, Indiana 46901
U.S.A.

ISBN 978-0-6151-3769-8
Copyright 2005 by Ray Freeman Ministries
All rights reserved
No portion of this book may be reproduced, stored in a retrieval system, or transmitted in any form or by any means electronic, mechanical photocopy, recording, or any other except for brief quotations in printed reviews, without the prior permission of the Publisher.

Contents

1. The Need to understand the Problem 7

2. Three spirits that control man 17

3. Do Demons Actually Exist? 29

4. Deliverance - What Does it Mean? 39

5. Bible Evidence of Curses 49

6. Self-Inflected Curses 61

7. Generational Curses 71

8. First Bind the Strong Man 79

9. Exposing the Deeds of Darkness 89

10. Demon spirits cause Sickness and Disease 103

11. Getting and Keeping the Victory over the Enemy..... 111

Introduction

This book is written to try and help the soldiers of the Cross fight the good fight of faith. It is hoped that it will assist responsible Christians in the exercise of the ministry of deliverance within the body of Christ, and also impart a new level of understanding and maturity to those who seek to walk as good soldiers of Christ Jesus.

We are in a war, and as BELIEVERS, we are to wage war on the enemy of our soul which is Satan and his demon spirits. Much of what is written in this book may be revelational because so many Christians don't even believe that there are demon spirits at work in the world today, let alone casting them out.

Christians are to wage war in the realm of the spirit-world and overthrow the strongholds of deception and ignorance and when that happens, it is like scales being removed from the eyes of the blinded.

There are those who say we shouldn't teach about demon powers or even talk about what they are and can do, but the fact is that the television screens and secular bookstores are full of dangerous, unclean material that is opening the minds of people to the spirit world, and as believers, we must understand how to deal with them.

Dr. Ray Freeman

The Need to Understand the Problem

Chapter 1

Clarifying of Terms

You can imagine how hard it is for the world to understand what we are talking about when 90% of Christians don't even understand it. A large part of the Christian church doesn't even believe in demon possession. So the first thing we need to understand is TERMS.

Antichrist

> **1 John 4:1-6**
> *"Beloved, believe not every spirit, but try the spirits whether they are of God: because many false prophets are gone out into the world. ²Hereby know ye the Spirit of God: Every spirit that confesseth that Jesus Christ is come in the flesh is of God: ³And every spirit that confesseth not that Jesus Christ is come in the flesh is not of God: and this is that spirit of antichrist, whereof ye have heard that it should come; and even now already is it in the world. ⁴Ye are of God, little children, and have overcome them: because greater is he that is in you, than he that is in the world. ⁵They are of the world: therefore speak they of the world, and the world heareth them. ⁶We are of God: he that knoweth God heareth us; he that is not of God heareth not us. Hereby know we the spirit of truth, and the spirit of error."*

The term "antichrist" does not mean what many think it means. The meaning is much broader than most understand. It means, *"instead of Christ."* While it does mean "against Christ" it goes much farther. Even the Muslims believe that there was a man named Jesus, and they do believe He was crucified, but they don't believe that He was the Son of God. They do believe He was a prophet sent from God. There are many spirits in this world today who will give some position of esteem to Jesus, but they will never acknowledge Him as the Son of God.

This is where so many Christians are going to be deceived. They are looking for a head-on battle not one masked in tolerance and seems friendly. What we need to understand is that **anything that takes the place of Christ in a man or woman's life is an antichrist.**

Occult

The Occult world places no value on the death and resurrection of Jesus Christ, but like all other antichrist spirits of the last days, they thrive on the supernatural. Many of them will say that they believe in Christ, like the Mormons or Jehovah Witness, but they don't believe that He is the Son of God. They may use the same word or term as Christians, but it doesn't mean the same. In dealing with the occult one had better know just what they really mean. Make them define their terms to you. You can say the same thing but it means something different.

Exorcism

This word is only used two times in the New Testament and each time it was dealing with the unregenerate:

Acts 19:13
"Then certain of the vagabond Jews, exorcists, took upon them to call over them which had evil spirits the name of the Lord Jesus, saying, We adjure you by Jesus whom Paul preacheth."

These people were not believers so they didn't have the authority to cast out demons in the Name of Jesus, and even the demons knew it.

Matthew 26:63
"But Jesus held his peace. And the high priest answered and said unto him, I adjure thee by the living God, that thou tell us whether thou be the Christ, the Son of God."

The High Priest used the words, *"I adjure (exorcise) you."* This was at the trial of Jesus before the Sanhedrin; once again, it was unbelievers trying to do something that they had no power to do.

If you will look closely at the word, the true meaning would be more, **"to swear or affirm by an oath, to administer an oath to, to adjure."** So the word **"exorcism"** is not a suitable word to describe the Christian's deliverance from the powers of darkness, but would perhaps apply more to what a **witch-doctor, a medium or occultists** would do with the co-operation of spirits by appeasement and sacrifices.

Having said that, we need to be aware that occultists will use any name, even the Name of Jesus, to obtain the results they seek from the powers of darkness. You may ask, "How can that happen?" **Matthew 7:21-23** *"Not every one that saith unto me, Lord, Lord, shall enter into the kingdom of heaven; but he that doeth the will of my*

Father which is in heaven. ²²Many will say to me in that day, Lord, Lord, have we not prophesied in thy name? and in thy name have cast out devils? and in thy name done many wonderful works? ²³And then will I profess unto them, I never knew you: depart from me, ye that work iniquity." It is clear from Scripture that demon spirits know the Name of Jesus and will respond to it no matter who uses it.

Let me explain it this way. An ungodly person can use the laws of God to reap a material harvest, but such temporal success counts for nothing when we stand before the Throne of God on judgment day.

There is a difference between pagan/occult exorcism even when it was practiced by the first century Jews and Christians. *"And when the unclean spirit had torn him, and cried with a loud voice, he came out of him. ²⁷And they were all amazed, insomuch that they questioned among themselves, saying, What thing is this? what new doctrine is this? for with authority commandeth he even the unclean spirits, and they do obey him. ²⁸And immediately his fame spread abroad throughout all the region round about Galilee" (Mark 1:26-28).* NOTE, Jesus did not appease like the Jewish exorcists – He commanded.

If the Church has a problem in making a distinction between occult exorcism and Christian deliverance, then how can we expect the world to understand?

Acts 19:13
"Then certain of the vagabond Jews, exorcists, took upon them to call over them which had evil spirits the name of the Lord Jesus, saying, We adjure you by Jesus whom Paul preacheth."

These people were not believers so they didn't have the authority to cast out demons in the Name of Jesus, and even the demons knew it.

Matthew 26:63
"But Jesus held his peace. And the high priest answered and said unto him, I adjure thee by the living God, that thou tell us whether thou be the Christ, the Son of God."

The High Priest used the words, *"I adjure (exorcise) you."* This was at the trial of Jesus before the Sanhedrin; once again, it was unbelievers trying to do something that they had no power to do.

If you will look closely at the word, the true meaning would be more, **"to swear or affirm by an oath, to administer an oath to, to adjure."** So the word **"exorcism"** is not a suitable word to describe the Christian's deliverance from the powers of darkness, but would perhaps apply more to what a **witch-doctor, a medium or occultists** would do with the co-operation of spirits by appeasement and sacrifices.

Having said that, we need to be aware that occultists will use any name, even the Name of Jesus, to obtain the results they seek from the powers of darkness. You may ask, "How can that happen?" **Matthew 7:21-23** *"Not every one that saith unto me, Lord, Lord, shall enter into the kingdom of heaven; but he that doeth the will of my*

Father which is in heaven. ²²Many will say to me in that day, Lord, Lord, have we not prophesied in thy name? and in thy name have cast out devils? and in thy name done many wonderful works? ²³And then will I profess unto them, I never knew you: depart from me, ye that work iniquity." It is clear from Scripture that demon spirits know the Name of Jesus and will respond to it no matter who uses it.

Let me explain it this way. An ungodly person can use the laws of God to reap a material harvest, but such temporal success counts for nothing when we stand before the Throne of God on judgment day.

There is a difference between pagan/occult exorcism even when it was practiced by the first century Jews and Christians. *"And when the unclean spirit had torn him, and cried with a loud voice, he came out of him. ²⁷And they were all amazed, insomuch that they questioned among themselves, saying, What thing is this? what new doctrine is this? for with authority commandeth he even the unclean spirits, and they do obey him. ²⁸And immediately his fame spread abroad throughout all the region round about Galilee" (Mark 1:26-28).* NOTE, Jesus did not appease like the Jewish exorcists – He commanded.

If the Church has a problem in making a distinction between occult exorcism and Christian deliverance, then how can we expect the world to understand?

Deliverance (Casting out Demon spirits)

Deliverance is for those who have been involved with the spirit of antichrist on some level, but now they are turning back to Christ, seeking to be free of every chain and weight the devil has put on them. **This was basic training for the disciples,** *"And when he had called unto him his twelve disciples, he gave them power against unclean spirits, to cast them out, and to heal all manner of sickness and all manner of disease" (Matthew. 10:1),* and it was carried forward until the close of the New Testament age, *"Teaching them to observe all things whatsoever I have commanded you: and, lo, I am with you alway, even unto the end of the world. Amen" (Matthew 28:20).*

It is difficult for me to see how any pastor or Christian can deny the relevance of casting out evil spirits today, unless they would also deny the Great Commission.

Deliverance is the most common term used by Christians when referring to casting out demons. We say it in the Lord's Prayer, *"... and lead us not into temptation, but deliver us from evil (or the evil one)" (Matt. 6:13).* One translation says, *"But rescue us from evil (or, the evil one)."*

Deliverance is not an addition to the gospel – it is not a by-product of the gospel – but it is an integral part of the gospel message. It is appropriating the FULL GOSPEL OF SALVATION for the Body, Soul, and Spirit.

Spirit

There are three spirits that control man, **the Spirit of God, the spirit of Satan, and the spirit of flesh or**

man. In the New Testament the Greek word is **"pneuma"** meaning wind or spirit. When God made man He breathed his (man's) spirit into him and he became a living soul. The angels are called *"ministering spirits"* and Satan's demons are described as *"unclean spirits"* and the demons themselves have spirits:

Luke 4:33
"And in the synagogue there was a man, which had a spirit of an unclean devil, and cried out with a loud voice,"

Revelation 16:14
"For they are the spirits of devils, working miracles, which go forth unto the kings of the earth and of the whole world, to gather them to the battle of that great day of God Almighty."

Jesus compared the Holy Spirit to the wind, *"The wind bloweth where it listeth, and thou hearest the sound thereof, but canst not tell whence it cometh, and whither it goeth: so is every one that is born of the Spirit" (John 3:8),* and is the person of the Godhead Who energises God's purpose and executes His will in Jesus' Name.

Many times you can discern the activity of unclean spirits by a cold atmosphere, and of course there are many other ways of discerning the presence of evil spirits that I will discuss later on in this study. The one thing that you need to understand is, that things are not what Hollywood tries to make them seem. While there are severe cases the good news is that most unclean spirits coming against Christians are not very strong. If we have the God kind of faith and the faith of the Son of God we can overcome.

Mark 11:22
"And Jesus answering saith unto them, Have faith in God (the God Kind of faith)."

Galatians 2:20
"I am crucified with Christ: nevertheless I live; yet not I, but Christ liveth in me: and the life which I now live in the flesh I live by the faith of the Son of God, who loved me, and gave himself for me."

The Holy Spirit is the breath of God; at death the human spirit leaves the body as a breath (reversing Genesis 2:7) and the substance of an unclean spirit is also a breath. In over 44 years of ministry I have seen many unclean spirits leave the human body with a yawn or cough or sneeze. They are expelled; thrust out as breaths in the same way that the body throws out poisonous waste products such as carbon dioxide.

Ezekiel 37:9
"Then said he unto me, Prophesy unto the wind, prophesy, son of man, and say to the wind, Thus saith the Lord GOD; Come from the four winds, O breath, and breathe upon these slain, that they may live."

John 20:22
"And when he had said this, he breathed on them, and saith unto them, Receive ye the Holy Ghost:"

This may seem strange to many, but stop and think, when the Spirit of the Lord is moving in a service and you look around and see people yawning or coughing or just plain looking uncomfortable, many times it's because of spirit in them.

Manifestation

Very simply, this word describes the way an unclean spirit reveals itself, or departs. Manifestations are many and varied, from aches and pains to sweating and limpness. There are many who don't have any manifestations at all but they still need deliverance and when they receive it, all that there is, is peace, a feeling of well-being.

I have seen it from the wild to absolutely nothing. Many make the mistake in believing that the wilder the reactions the more demons that a person has, but that's not so. Just as some people can't put up with much pressure without falling "apart," there are people who just can't handle any kind of spiritual invasion without having a reaction. This is also true with Christians, the Holy Spirit fills them and they have a reaction and go wild, while others may speak in tongues but have very little other manifestations. We forget that each one of us are wonderfully made by God and we each have our own physical reactions to different kinds of things.

It is wrong to attempt to measure a demonized person by the manifestations. In fact the Spirit Filled believer, when attacked by demon spirits, may have a greater reaction than a sinner person. Why? Because it is an alien power trying to come into them and the Holy Spirit in them recognizes what is going on, but physically they can have a reaction.

The question is asked, can a believer be demon possessed or demonized? Of course the answer is NO! But they can and are attacked by demons.

NOTE:
Some teach that every Christian is filled with the Spirit, the basis of this teaching is the flimsiest textual evidence imaginable, totally misinterpreting Ephesians 5:18 *"And be not drunk with wine, wherein is excess; but be filled with the Spirit,"* and Colossian 2:10 *"And ye are complete in him, which is the head of all principality and power."* They teach that if we are sealed with the Holy Spirit we are AUTOMATICALLY FILLED with the Spirit. If that is the case then why in Acts 6:3 when they were selecting deacons that one of the conditions was that they be *"Full of the Spirit"*? *"Wherefore, brethren, look ye out among you seven men of honest report, full of the Holy Ghost and wisdom, whom we may appoint over this business" (Acts 6:3).* If everybody if filled with the Holy Spirit why would they be sorting people out because of it?

16

Three Spirits That Can Control Man

Chapter 2

To hear many talk, everything that we see and even the earth we live on just happened. Billions of years ago something happened, they don't really know what or where, but something. The truth is that our universe is no accident. D.L. Moody said**, "If you can believe the first verse of the Bible you should have no problem believing everything else."**

Genesis 1:1
In the beginning God created the heaven and the earth.

"In the beginning God (Elohim)" tells us about the power and greatness of our God. God stepped out on nothing and took nothing and made everything from it. What a mighty God. The earth is just a small part of what God created, for everything in this universe was created by Him and for Him.

God's Power

When we try to explain the power of God we just don't have the words to tell just how much power He really has because it has never really been tested.

The question is asked, "How do we really know that God exists?" The answer can be given in two parts: First, all people have an inner sense of God. Second, we believe the evidence that is found in Scripture and in nature.

No matter where we go on this planet people worship some kind of God, they may not have ever heard the Gospel but they still believe in some god and worship them. Then we have the Bible which is one of if not the oldest record of man's history on this earth. How many books can be traced back over 3,000 years?

Isaiah 64:8
*But now, O L*ORD*, thou art our father; we are the clay, and thou our potter; and we all are the work of thy hand.*

Acts 10:38
How God anointed Jesus of Nazareth with the Holy Ghost and with power: who went about doing good, and healing all that were oppressed of the devil; for God was with him.

Hebrews 1:1
God, who at sundry times and in divers manners spake in time past unto the fathers by the prophets.

The apostle Paul said that even the Gentile unbelievers *"knew God"* but did not honor him as God or give thanks to him. *"Because that, when they knew God, they glorified him not as God, neither were thankful; but became vain in their imaginations, and their foolish heart was darkened" (Romans 1:21).* He went on to say they are those, *"Who changed the truth of God into a lie, and worshipped and served the creature more than the Creator, who is blessed for ever. Amen" (Romans 1:25).* Paul is implying that they actively or willfully rejected some truth about God's existence and character that they knew. Romans 1:19 tells us that they knew it because God showed it to them, *"for God hath shewed it unto them."*

The Bible calls those who reject or deny that God exists, *"fools."*

Psalm 14:1
The fool hath said in his heart, There is no God. They are corrupt, they have done abominable works, there is none that doeth good.

The Apostle Paul also recognized that people will deny the knowledge of God because of sin, **Romans 1:18** *"For the wrath of God is revealed from heaven against all ungodliness and unrighteousness of men, who hold the truth in unrighteousness (or suppress truth)."* He went on to say that they are *"without excuse" (Romans 1:20).*

The Spirit of Man

The spirit of man is so often overlooked. Not only is there the Spirit of God that can control us, but the spirit of man or flesh. When God made man it says, *"And the LORD God formed man of the dust of the ground, and breathed into his nostrils the breath of life; and man became a living soul" (Genesis 2:7).* In making man God gave him a will of his own. Man is not made, forced, to serve God, he must decide.

Romans 6:16
Know ye not, that to whom ye yield yourselves servants to obey, his servants ye are to whom ye obey; whether of sin unto death, or of obedience unto righteousness?

Because man is a **"free moral agent"** he has the power or right to choose who or if he will worship. Satan can not make man worship or serve him, and God will not make him serve Him either, it's a choice.

What does Scripture mean about the "soul" and "spirit" man? In Genesis chapters one and two we find that it says, *"And God said, Let us make man in our image, after our likeness" (Genesis 1:26).* Just as the One Supreme God is a trinity, Father, Son, and Holy Spirit, so man is also a tri-unity, **Body, Soul, and Spirit.**

Many forget that man is a spirit being that lives in a body and has an eternal soul. Satan can and does use the spirit of flesh to cause us to sin. When we yield our selves to sin it is because Satan has tempted us and we have yielded. In other words, we make the decision to do or not to do. It's what is called being a "free moral agent." Even God does not violate man's "will." He comes and knocks on our heart's door, but it is up to us to answer.

The spirit tells us to breath, eat, and sleep, our heart to beat and so on. Many times we blame things on the devil when it is just us, for instance, being lazy. Satan can and does use those things but we let him. Look at it this way, the spirit of man is a neutral power with the potential to become a part of the good or the bad.

Romans 6:16
Know ye not, that to whom ye yield yourselves servants to obey, his servants ye are to whom ye obey; whether of sin unto death, or of obedience unto righteousness?

Someone asked what is sin? Sin is any failure to conform to the moral law of God in act, attitude, or nature.

The Spirit of Satan (Lucifer)

The devil is a malicious personality who seeks to destroy God's work and man's life. He tried to lead a revolt in heaven and was kicked out because of it. He is not just an influence or an idea that weak minds have dreamed up. He is a real person. Even through he was kicked out of heaven he still is a person, of the keenest personalities ever created. Yes! He was and is a created being! Even Michael, the Archangel refused to rebuke Satan in the dispute over the body of Moses. *"Yet Michael the archangel, when contending with the devil he disputed about the body of Moses, durst not bring against him a railing accusation, but said, The Lord rebuke thee" (Jude 1:9).*

Satan is his personal name. *"Now there was a day when the sons of God came to present themselves before the LORD, and Satan came also among them" (Job 1:6).* Here he appears as the enemy of God who brings severe temptations against Job because Job loved and served God.

Isaiah 14:12
How art thou fallen from heaven, O Lucifer, son of the morning! How art thou cut down to the ground, which didst weaken the nations!

Isaiah 14:13
For thou hast said in thine heart, I will ascend into heaven, I will exalt my throne above the stars of God: I will sit also upon the mount of the congregation, in the sides of the north:

Isaiah 14:14
I will ascend above the heights of the clouds; I will be like the most High.

We have the story of the fall, the works and destiny of Satan in the Bible.

Ezekiel 28:12
Son of man, take up a lamentation upon the king of Tyrus, and say unto him, Thus saith the Lord GOD; Thou sealest up the sum, full of wisdom, and perfect in beauty.

Ezekiel 28:13
Thou hast been in Eden the garden of God; every precious stone was thy covering, the sardius, topaz, and the diamond, the beryl, the onyx, and the jasper, the sapphire, the emerald, and the carbuncle, and gold: the workmanship of thy tabrets and of thy pipes was prepared in thee in the day that thou wast created.

Ezekiel 28:14
Thou art the anointed cherub that covereth; and I have set thee so: thou wast upon the holy mountain of God; thou hast walked up and down in the midst of the stones of fire.

Ezekiel 28:15
Thou wast perfect in thy ways from the day that thou wast created, till iniquity was found in thee.

Ezekiel 28:16
By the multitude of thy merchandise they have filled the midst of thee with violence, and thou hast sinned: therefore I will cast thee as profane out of the mountain of God: and I will destroy thee, O covering cherub, from the midst of the stones of fire.

Ezekiel 28:17
Thine heart was lifted up because of thy beauty, thou hast corrupted thy wisdom by reason of thy brightness: I will cast thee to the ground, I will lay thee before kings, that they may behold thee.

Ezekiel 28:18
Thou hast defiled thy sanctuaries by the multitude of thine iniquities, by the iniquity of thy traffick; therefore will I bring forth a fire from the midst of thee, it shall devour thee, and I will bring thee to ashes upon the earth in the sight of all them that behold thee.

Ezekiel 28:19
All they that know thee among the people shall be astonished at thee: thou shalt be a terror, and never shalt thou be any more.

Satan was not content with being one of the most powerful angels in heaven. He was not content to be beautiful and intelligent. Satan wanted to be equal with God. If you look closely it would seem that his contest was with the Jesus Christ, although the entire Godhead was challenged.

The battle that took place in heaven is now on the earth and will not be over until Satan is finally cast into the lake of fire forever and ever.

Satan was created by God as one of the highest order of angels. Ezekiel 28:12 could only be applied to a supernatural being and not just an ordinary man who ruled on earth.

> **Lucifer (Satan) was one of three archangels or Generals of the host of heaven; the others were Michael and Gabriel. Lucifer was the praise and worship leader of heaven (Ezekiel 28:13). Michael was the war angel (Revelation 12:7, while Gabriel was the messenger of God (Luke 1:19, 26). It would seem that these three Archangels were to govern and administer the will of God. They carried out the desires of God-the-Father to the other Angels of heaven and after God made the earth and mankind, here on earth. Satan was not content with being one of the most powerful angels of heaven he wanted to be the most powerful.**

What a gorgeous creature he must have been, but it was his beauty that filled him with pride and caused him to fall. Look at some of his abilities and titles:

➢ He was called *"the cherub that covereth."*

➢ He was the first being with musical ability.

- There is now documented evidence that heavy metal rock music has seduced and is seducing young people. Musical instruments were originally designed to be a means of praising and worshiping God. Satan had a built-in pipe organ, or he was an organ, that is what is meant by, "the workmanship of thy tabrets and thy pipes…"

➢ Even in his fallen state, he still has great power. **Jude 1:9 *"Yet Michael the archangel, when contending with the devil he disputed about the body of Moses, durst not bring against him a railing accusation, but*** *said, The Lord rebuke thee."* Michael the archangel refuse to rebuke him but said, *"The Lord rebuke thee."*

One of the most important things that you can ever learn is that Satan is not an influence or an idea, he is a real person. *"Be sober, be vigilant; because your adversary the devil, as a roaring lion, walketh about, seeking whom he may devour" (1 Peter 5:8).*

Satan is not just an influence or an ideal that weak minds have dreamed up. He is a real being. Yes! He is a created being! Even Michael, the Archangel refused to rebuke Satan in the dispute over the body of Moses. WHY? Because they were both created beings. *"Yet Michael the archangel, when contending with the devil he disputed about the body of Moses, durst not bring against him a railing accusation, but said, The Lord rebuke thee" (Jude 1:9).*

> **This brings up the following question. Why didn't Michael rebuke him? Because they were both created beings, created with the same power, but he did say, *"The Lord rebuke thee" (Jude 1:9).***

Satan appears as the enemy of God who brings severe temptations against Job. Also in the life of David, King of Israel, it was Satan that caused David to number Israel (1 Chronicles 21:1), which was against what God had told David to do. The name **"Satan"** means **"adversary."** The English translation of the name **"devil"** is **diabolos,"** which means **"slanderer."**

Satan as we know him came on the scene in Genesis 3:1 *"Now the serpent was more subtil than any beast of the field which the LORD God had made. And he said unto the woman, Yea, hath God said, Ye shall not eat of every tree of the garden?"* You will note that even in his first appearance he needed a body before he could speak out into this earthly realm. Many forget that Satan is a spirit being who had no rights on the earth. He chooses a serpent to use to speak through which brought a curse upon the serpent, **Genesis 3:14** *"Because thou hast done this, thou art cursed above all cattle, and above every beast of the field; upon thy belly shalt thou go, and dust shalt thou eat all the days of thy life:"*

> **The first created thing that Satan touched became cursed and remains cursed to this day.**

The question asked, why did Satan need to use the serpent? Because as a spirit being he could not speak out into this earthly realm, Jesus, who is the Son of the Living God needed a body to come into this earthly economy, *"Wherefore when he cometh into the world, he saith, Sacrifice and offering thou wouldest not, but a body hast thou prepared me:" (Hebrews 10:5).*

> **You will note that Jesus did no miracles after the resurrection, because He was in a spiritual body. I'm not saying that Jesus couldn't, I'm saying He submitted Himself to the laws of God as the Son of God while He was in the flesh and also after he received His glorified body.**

Adam was the head authority on this planet. Everything that moved was under his control, he could have, and should have told Satan to get off this planet, and Satan would have had to go. Satan was an intruder from the beginning.

Genesis 1:28
And God blessed them, and God said unto them, Be fruitful, and multiply, and replenish the earth, and subdue it: and have dominion over the fish of the sea, and over the fowl of the air, and over every living thing that moveth upon the earth.

NOTE: Here is the lesson that we must learn from Genesis:

- Satan is an outsider, meaning he has no rights or power other than what we give him. If Adam had done what he should have, then Satan could not have done anything. But Adam surrendered his rights into the hands of Satan.

- Satan can only work when he has a body to work through. Because he has no rights, he needs someone else to do his work for him. If only Christians would stop allowing themselves to be used by the devil.

The question is asked, when do we stop being a Christian and go back into the bondage of Satan or, can you? **Romans 6:16** *"Know ye not, that to whom ye yield yourselves servants to <u>obey</u>, his servants ye are to whom ye <u>obey</u>; whether of sin unto death, or of obedience unto righteousness?"* <u>ALL DISOBEDANCE IS OF THE DEVIL.</u> The Bible is clear on this subject, you can't serve two masters, so the minute we become disobedient to God, Satan becomes our master. I know that what I'm saying is hard, but read the Word of God for yourself. God is not in partnership with Satan.

While we don't know just when Lucifer (Satan) sinned we do know that it was in heaven, and it was the sin of pride, and it was before God created man. And we do know as Satan he is **John 8:44** *"He was a murderer from the beginning, and abode not in the truth, because there is no truth in him. When he speaketh a lie, he speaketh of his own: for he is a liar, and the father of it."* In John 3:8 it says that Satan, *"He that committeth sin is of the devil; for the devil sinneth from the beginning"* The *"from the beginning"* is from the beginning of time and time didn't start until God began His creation of the earth.

1 Peter 5:8

Be sober, be vigilant; because your adversary the devil, as a roaring lion, walketh about, seeking whom he may devour:

Ephesians 6:10-12

Finally, my brethren, be strong in the Lord, and in the power of his might. ¹¹Put on the whole armour of God, that ye may be able to stand against the wiles of the devil. ¹²For we wrestle not against flesh and blood, but against principalities, against powers, against the rulers of the darkness of this world, against spiritual wickedness in high places.

Do Demons Actually Exist?

Chapter 3

Luke 4:18-20
The Spirit of the Lord is upon me, because he hath anointed me to preach the gospel to the poor; he hath sent me to heal the brokenhearted, to preach deliverance to the captives, and recovering of sight to the blind, to set at liberty them that are bruised, To preach the acceptable year of the Lord. And he closed the book, and he gave it again to the minister, and sat down. And the eyes of all them that were in the synagogue were fastened on him.

In today's world there are so many who ask, **"Do demons actually exist? Or do they belong to the world of myth, and folklore, and the delusions of demented or superstitious people who are unenlightened by modern science?"** There are so many religious leaders who think that any supernatural activity is better explained by psychology or at least in physiological terms, and that belief in the devil is dated and should be left in the past.

C.S. Lewis, in his classic book, *The Screwtape Letters,* which describes demonic strategy, predicted the rise of a strange mixture of science and religion. The book is written in the form a series of letters from a senior demon (Screwtape) to a junior demon (Wormwood). In the seventh letter, Screwtape describes what he sees as a promising trend in modern society.

"Our policy for the moment is to conceal ourselves. Of course this has not always been so. We are

really faced with a cruel dilemma. When the humans disbelieve our existence we lose all the pleasing results of direct terrorism, and we make no magicians. On the other hand, when they believe in us, we cannot make them materialists or skeptics. At least not yet. I have great hopes that we shall learn in due time how to emotionalize and mythologize their science to such an extent that which is, in effect, a belief in us (though not under that name) will creep in while the human mind remains closed to the belief in the enemy. The "LIFE FORCE," the worship of sex, and some aspects of psychoanalysis may here prove useful.

For the answer to our question we must ultimately go to the Bible. The New Testament clearly teaches the existence of both Satan and demons.

Luke 10:17
And the seventy returned again with joy, saying, Lord, even the devils are subject unto us through thy name.

Revelation 12:7
And there was war in heaven: Michael and his angels fought against the dragon; and the dragon fought and his angels,

Revelation 12:8
And prevailed not; neither was their place found any more in heaven.

Revelation 12:9
And the great dragon was cast out, that old serpent, called the Devil, and Satan, which deceiveth the whole world: he was cast out into the earth, and his angels were cast out with him.

Revelation 12:10
And I heard a loud voice saying in heaven, Now is come salvation, and strength, and the kingdom of our God, and the power of his Christ: for the accuser of our brethren is cast down, which accused them before our God day and night.

A close study of the life of Jesus shows that His ministry was marked by continual confrontations with demons and He gave authority to His followers to cast them out, *"Then he called his twelve disciples together, and gave them power and authority over all devils, and to cure diseases" (Luke 9:1).* The Apostle Paul taught that the believer has authority over demons. If our Lord and the Apostle Paul taught that demons were real, I believe they knew what they were taking about.

Ephesians 6:10
Finally, my brethren, be strong in the Lord, and in the power of his might.

Ephesians 6:11
Put on the whole armour of God, that ye may be able to stand against the wiles of the devil.

Ephesians 6:12
For we wrestle not against flesh and blood, but against principalities, against powers, against the rulers of the darkness of this world, against spiritual wickedness in high places.

Ephesians 6:13
Wherefore take unto you the whole armour of God, that ye may be able to withstand in the evil day, and having done all, to stand.

Ephesians 6:14
Stand therefore, having your loins girt about with truth, and having on the breastplate of righteousness;

Ephesians 6:15
And your feet shod with the preparation of the gospel of peace;

Ephesians 6:16
Above all, taking the shield of faith, wherewith ye shall be able to quench all the fiery darts of the wicked.

Ephesians 6:17
And take the helmet of salvation, and the sword of the Spirit, which is the word of God:

Ephesians 6:18
Praying always with all prayer and supplication in the Spirit, and watching thereunto with all perseverance and supplication for all saints;

Ephesians 6:19
And for me, that utterance may be given unto me, that I may open my mouth boldly, to make known the mystery of the gospel,

Colossians 1:13
Who hath delivered us from the power of darkness, and hath translated us into the kingdom of his dear Son:

The Apostle Paul tells us just how we overcome the power of the devil. As believers we have the same kind of faith that Jesus had (Mark 11:22) and because of that we are made to set with Him in heavenly places. We now have become joint-heirs with Jesus Christ, which means we are not waiting to receive in the sweet by-and-by but in the present we have power over all the powers of this world.

Colossians 1:14
In whom we have redemption through his blood, even the forgiveness of sins:

Colossians 1:15
Who is the image of the invisible God, the firstborn of every creature:

Colossians 1:16
For by him were all things created, that are in heaven, and that are in earth, visible and invisible, whether they be thrones, or dominions, or principalities, or powers: all things were created by him, and for him:

There is undeniable evidence of demons throughout the history of the early church. All of the early church fathers and all of the reformers believed the devil exists and that his works manifest among us. Human experiences testify of the devil's existence. Anyone who walks in victory does so because they have overcome the powers of the devil.

How Does Evil Spirits Affect Us?

Because as Christians we become identified with Christ, Satan has made us a prime target, *"**Beloved, think it not strange concerning the fiery trial which is to try you, as though some strange thing happened unto you: But rejoice, inasmuch as ye are partakers of Christ's sufferings; that, when his glory shall be revealed, ye may be glad also with exceeding joy" (1 Peter 4:12-13).*** Most

Christians don't realize that they live in a war zone, but they do. The kingdom of Satan is powerful and well organized and it affects men and women in many different ways.

Satan Attacks Us In Three (3) Ways:

1. **Temptation** – Almost all temptations are the results of our own choices and the influence of the world:

    Jeremiah 17:9
    The heart is deceitful above all things, and desperately wicked: who can know it?

    Mark 7:20
    And he said, That which cometh out of the man, that defileth the man.

    Mark 7:21
    For from within, out of the heart of men, proceed evil thoughts, adulteries, fornications, murders,

    Mark 7:22
    Thefts, covetousness, wickedness, deceit, lasciviousness, an evil eye, blasphemy, pride, foolishness:

    Mark 7:23
    All these evil things come from within, and defile the man.

    James 1:14
    But every man is tempted, when he is drawn away of his own lust, and enticed.

James 1:15
Then when lust hath conceived, it bringeth forth sin: and sin, when it is finished, bringeth forth death.

The Scriptures describe a second category of temptations that involves a more direct demonic influence. For example, Satan directly tempted Christ in the wilderness (Matthew 4:1-11); he tempted Ananias to lie about his personal finances (Acts 5:3); and he incited David to sin by taking a census in Israel (1 Chronicles 21:1). The world, the flesh, and the devil work in concerted efforts to tempt us. They have a diabolical interrelationship that seeks to trap men and women in sin and death. When we yield to the temptations of the flesh and the world, we become more vulnerable to further demonic temptations, because Satan knows if it worked once it will work again.

2. **Opposition** – Some think that because they are called by God to preach, teach, or become a missionary, that Satan will let them alone. SORRY! I wish it worked that way, but it doesn't. Satan and his evil spirits work overtime in trying to prevent the preaching of the Gospel of the kingdom. The apostle Peter warned us, ***"Think it not strange" (1 Peter 4:12)***, in other words, for Satan not to attack would be strange.

Opposition can come in many different forms, sickness, or by causing an accident, or by causing those who work for you to find fault, there are many ways.

In Daniel's day we can see clearly the influence of demonic spirits. There was a powerful demonic spirit that ruled over Persia, and by the way, it still does, and Daniel prayed 21 days without an answer. When the Angel of the

Lord did come, the Angel related the story of the battle with demon spirits:

> **Daniel 10:12-13**
> *Then said he unto me, Fear not, Daniel: for from the first day that thou didst set thine heart to understand, and to chasten thyself before thy God, thy words were heard, and I am come for thy words. But the prince of the kingdom of Persia withstood me one and twenty days: but, lo, Michael, one of the chief princes, came to help me; and I remained there with the kings of Persia.*

Also look at Paul's ministry (Acts 13:6-10). The magician opposing him, and the slave girl that had a spirit of divination (Acts 16:16-18) who caused a scene when Paul tried to preach.

3. **Possession/Demonization** – Satan and his demons may also attack men and women by getting a grip on their personal or physical lives. Unbelievers can be possessed or demonized. While Christians cannot be possessed they can be demonized or come under the control of demon spirits.

Many don't understand that because man is a free moral agent that demons, while they can possess a person, they can not absolutely control them at all times, which gives a place for deliverance and salvation. The problem is that Satan/demons can have such great control of people that it takes someone full of the Holy Spirit to deal with them.

> **Matthew 4:24**
> *And his fame went throughout all Syria: and they brought unto him all sick people that were taken*

with divers diseases and torments, and those which were possessed with devils, and those which were lunatick, and those that had the palsy; and he healed them.

Mark 1:32
And at even, when the sun did set, they brought unto him all that were diseased, and them that were possessed with devils.

Luke 8:36
They also which saw it told them by what means he that was possessed of the devils was healed.

John 10:21
Others said, These are not the words of him that hath a devil. Can a devil open the eyes of the blind?

The demonized suffer under varying degrees of bondage. They can be troubled in their thoughts or they can just have a reaction when they hear the Gospel preached. Who is demonized? Anyone who is under an attack by demons, it can be physically, mentally, and emotionally.

There are three steps into possession:

1. Oppression
2. Obsession
3. Possession

Deliverance – What Does It Mean?

Chapter 4

Mark 16:17
And these signs shall follow them that believe; In my name shall they cast out devils; they shall speak with new tongues;

Luke 4:18-19
The Spirit of the Lord is upon me, because he hath anointed me to preach the gospel to the poor; he hath sent me to heal the brokenhearted, to preach deliverance to the captives, and recovering of sight to the blind, to set at liberty them that are bruised, To preach the acceptable year of the Lord.

In the Book of Isaiah, the great Old Testament prophet describes the ministry of the coming Messiah as *"to proclaim liberty to the captives" (Isaiah 61:1).* In the New Testament when Jesus came back from the wilderness temptation He went into the Temple and said, *"The Spirit of the Lord is upon me, because he hath anointed me to preach the gospel to the poor; he hath sent me to heal the brokenhearted, to preach deliverance to the captives, and recovering of sight to the blind, to set at liberty them that are bruised, To preach the acceptable year of the Lord" (Luke 4:18-19).* How can anyone read the above and not believe that Jesus has already delivered us from the sins that separates us from our heavenly Father, from curses and bondage that the enemy, Satan, has inflicted on us?

1 John 3:8
He that committeth sin is of the devil; for the devil sinneth from the beginning. For this purpose the Son of God was manifested, that he might destroy the works of the devil. (Note this is from the beginning of time as we know it.)

When Jesus called the twelve disciples together, He gave them power and authority to drive demons out and to heal the sick. **NOTE,** they were sent to preach the kingdom of God and to heal the sick, *"Then he called his twelve disciples together, and gave them power and authority over all devils, and to cure diseases. And he sent them to preach the kingdom of God, and to heal the sick" (Luke 9:1-2).*

Please note that Jesus always combined the preaching of the Gospel with healing and casting out demon spirits, placing the importance of preaching the Gospel before that of healing or casting out demons.

The Entry Point

Demons gain a foothold in people's lives through a variety of ways. Basically, the main culprit is sin. The list is big and even though people know it they continue to be demonized.

Here are just a few of the entry points:

- **Unrighteous anger**
- **Self-hatred**
- **Hatred of others**
- **Revenge**

Deliverance – What Does It Mean?

Chapter 4

Mark 16:17
And these signs shall follow them that believe; In my name shall they cast out devils; they shall speak with new tongues;

Luke 4:18-19
The Spirit of the Lord is upon me, because he hath anointed me to preach the gospel to the poor; he hath sent me to heal the brokenhearted, to preach deliverance to the captives, and recovering of sight to the blind, to set at liberty them that are bruised, To preach the acceptable year of the Lord.

In the Book of Isaiah, the great Old Testament prophet describes the ministry of the coming Messiah as *"to proclaim liberty to the captives" (Isaiah 61:1).* In the New Testament when Jesus came back from the wilderness temptation He went into the Temple and said, *"The Spirit of the Lord is upon me, because he hath anointed me to preach the gospel to the poor; he hath sent me to heal the brokenhearted, to preach deliverance to the captives, and recovering of sight to the blind, to set at liberty them that are bruised, To preach the acceptable year of the Lord" (Luke 4:18-19).* How can anyone read the above and not believe that Jesus has already delivered us from the sins that separates us from our heavenly Father, from curses and bondage that the enemy, Satan, has inflicted on us?

1 John 3:8
He that committeth sin is of the devil; for the devil sinneth from the beginning. For this purpose the Son of God was manifested, that he might destroy the works of the devil. (Note this is from the beginning of time as we know it.)

When Jesus called the twelve disciples together, He gave them power and authority to drive demons out and to heal the sick. **NOTE,** they were sent to preach the kingdom of God and to heal the sick, *"Then he called his twelve disciples together, and gave them power and authority over all devils, and to cure diseases. And he sent them to preach the kingdom of God, and to heal the sick" (Luke 9:1-2).*

Please note that Jesus always combined the preaching of the Gospel with healing and casting out demon spirits, placing the importance of preaching the Gospel before that of healing or casting out demons.

The Entry Point

Demons gain a foothold in people's lives through a variety of ways. Basically, the main culprit is sin. The list is big and even though people know it they continue to be demonized.

Here are just a few of the entry points:

- **Unrighteous anger**
- **Self-hatred**
- **Hatred of others**
- **Revenge**

- Unforgiveness
- Lust
- Pornography
- Sexual perversions
- Drugs
- Alcohol

These open the door to demonic influence in our lives.

There is a verse of Scripture in Ecclesiastes 10:8 that we need to understand *"He that diggeth a pit shall fall into it; and whoso breaketh an hedge, a serpent shall bite him."* The phrase *"whoso breaketh an hedge"* is important, because as believers there is a hedge of God's protection around us and when we sin the hedge is broken and becomes an entry point for demons.

Please understand this; even non-believers have a hedge called their "free will." It is when they yield their free will to any sin that they open that hedge to allow demons to come in.

Our WILL is God's gift to all mankind. Satan can't do anything to us or through us unless we allow it. Even God can't save us against our WILL. Satan, through temptations, attacks the hedge of protection, but it is up to us not to yield. God, by the Holy Spirit, knocks on the door, but still it's up to us to answer, it's our free will to answer or not.

An opening must be made before demons can come into a person. It only takes a small entry point for a person to become demonized. Any sin will open the hedge and allow demons to come into a person's life. Just as a believer should be getting better and better each day of their life so the unbeliever should realize that even the least of sin, if there is such a thing, will grow daily. What starts out as something small, turns into a big sin. In other words, once the entry point has been established it never stays the same, it will grow larger and larger.

1. **Occultic Doorways** – The word occult literally means **"hidden"**, which clearly reveals how Satan orchestrates his plans to enter into a person's life. The occult always involves religious practices whose sources are not of God.

Deuteronomy 18:10
There shall not be found among you any one that maketh his son or his daughter to pass through the fire, or that useth divination, or an observer of times, or an enchanter, or a witch,

Deuteronomy 18:11
Or a charmer, or a consulter with familiar spirits, or a wizard, or a necromancer.

Deuteronomy 18:12
For all that do these things are an abomination unto the LORD: and because of these abominations the LORD thy God doth drive them out from before thee.

Deuteronomy 18:13
Thou shalt be perfect with the LORD thy God.

Deuteronomy 18:14
For these nations, which thou shalt possess, hearkened unto observers of times, and unto diviners: but as for thee, the LORD thy God hath not suffered thee so to do.

2 Kings 21:6
And he made his son pass through the fire, and observed times, and used enchantments, and dealt with familiar spirits and wizards: he wrought much wickedness in the sight of the LORD, to provoke him to anger.

HERE IS A LIST OF A FEW OCCULTIC PRACTICES TO BE AVOIDED:

- Horoscope reading
- Fortune telling
- Tea leaf and palm reading
- Consultation with people who have a familiar spirit.
- The use of ouija boards
- Talking to the dead
- Astrology (telling the future by observing the time, reading the stars)
- ESP (extra-sensory perception) or any psychic experiences
- Prayers and incantations with the use of candles
- Spells, levitation (floating in air) (moving of objects by means of mind control)

2. **New Age Doorway** – The New Age Movement is a worldwide religion which is an outright counterfeit of Christianity. Its teachings are so deceptive, often presented in the guise of scientific, medical, and even Christian; but in reality, these

are Hindu teachings and practices. New Age believes that God is an impersonal force, that the entire world and universe and everything within it, is God. They also believe in reincarnation and in karma.

Here is a list of New Age practices:

- Yoga, meaning "yoke" or "link." Most don't even know that they are being yoked or linked to demons.
- Meditation. To them, it's emptying the mind so that demon spirits could enter and control the person.
- This form of meditation is a counterfeit of what the Bible calls "meditation" in:

Joshua 1:8, *"This book of the law shall not depart out of thy mouth; but thou shalt meditate therein day and night, that thou mayest observe to do according to all that is written therein: for then thou shalt make thy way prosperous, and then thou shalt have good success."*

Or Psalms 119:9-11, *"Wherewithal shall a young man cleanse his way? by taking heed thereto according to thy word. With my whole heart have I sought thee: O let me not wander from thy commandments. Thy word have I hid in mine heart, that I might not sin against thee."*

- Mind control or hypnosis
- Acupuncture. This refers to the use of needles to numb the nerves.

3. **Childhood Doorways** – Few parents understand that there are traumatic and scary encounters with demons spirits during childhood...

   - Fear of monsters
   - Ghost friends and ghostly visitations
   - Repeated or recurring nightmares
   - Fear of scary toys
   - Cartoons

4. **Doorways of Inheritance – Or Inherited spirits** - What most believers don't understand is that many times demons and demonic bondages are inherited. The Bible strongly points out that the sins of the father will affect the generations that follow.

Exodus 20:5
"Thou shalt not bow down thyself to them, nor serve them: for I the LORD thy God am a jealous God, visiting the iniquity of the fathers upon the children unto the third and fourth generation of them that hate me"

Exodus 34:6-7
"And the LORD passed by before him, and proclaimed, The LORD, The LORD God, merciful and gracious, longsuffering, and abundant in goodness and truth, ⁷Keeping mercy for thousands, forgiving iniquity and transgression and sin, and that will by no means clear the guilty; visiting the iniquity of the fathers upon the children, and upon the children's children, unto the third and to the fourth generation.

<u>**Moses in his last message to Israel warned them about inherited spirits.**</u>

Deuteronomy 5:9

"Thou shalt not bow down thyself unto them, nor serve them: for I the LORD thy God am a jealous God, visiting the iniquity of the fathers upon the children unto the third and fourth generation of them that hate me"

Anyone who works with people will notice that certain family behaviors, both desirable and undesirable, are repetitive. Thus, a father who models discipline and faithfulness may install them in his children; on the other hand, if they are not faithful it also carries over into the children.

5. **Sexual Perversion** – Sex is God's gift to marriage. When it is practiced outside of marriage it is wrong. Young and old need to understand that any sex outside of marriage is a doorway to demon spirits. Listed below are sexual sins to be avoided:

    ➢ Adultery
    ➢ Fornication (pre-marital sex, trial marriages)
    ➢ Incest (between or among family members)
    ➢ Homosexuality and Lesbianism (Leviticus 18:22; Romans 1:26-32)
    ➢ Pornography and Fantasy (Matthew 6:22
    ➢ Abortion
    ➢ Sexual Abuse
    ➢ Bestiality (sex with animals)
    ➢ Transvestism (a man dressing up in woman's clothing) and trans-sexuality (not only dressing up in woman's clothing but wanting to be a member of the opposite sex, oftentimes involving sex transplant.)

6. **Doorway through Martial Arts** – What many don't know is that these arts were developed by a culture that is saturated with demon worship.

7. **Doorways through Rock Music** – Satan's music is often laced with subliminal, suggestive messages about rebellion, suicide, drug addiction, cursing, and sex.

8. **Doorways through Familiar Objects or Cursed Objects** –

    2 Chronicles 29:16
    "And the priests went into the inner part of the house of the LORD, to cleanse it, and brought out all the uncleanness that they found in the temple of the LORD into the court of the house of the LORD. And the Levites took it, to carry it out abroad into the brook Kidron."

    ➢ Idols

    Deuteronomy 7:25-26
    "The graven images of their gods shall ye burn with fire: thou shalt not desire the silver or gold that is on them, nor take it unto thee, lest thou be snared therein: for it is an abomination to the LORD thy God. Neither shalt thou bring an abomination into thine house, lest thou be a cursed thing like it: but thou shalt utterly detest it, and thou shalt utterly abhor it; for it is a cursed thing."

    1 Corinthians 10:19-20
    "What say I then? that the idol is any thing, or that which is offered in sacrifice to idols is any

thing? But I say, that the things which the Gentiles sacrifice, they sacrifice to devils, and not to God: and I would not that ye should have fellowship with devils."

- Amulets
- Cursed jewelry – many times this is how an inherited curse comes.
- Toys and games (with demonic images)

9. **Doorways through Addiction** – There are more lives destroyed because of addictions to drugs, drinks, cigarettes, etc.

If you have opened doorways to demons in your life whether deliberate or not, these must be closed. How? 1 John 1:9, *"If we confess our sins, he is faithful and just to forgive us our sins, and to cleanse us from all unrighteousness."* We need to come to God in true repentance, confess our sins and involvement to Him openly, accept His forgiveness and allow Him to cleanse us thoroughly with His Blood. But once this first step is done, we need to stay free by choosing to obey His Word and shunning all situations that might open up the protective hedge again. As our Lord Jesus said to the adulterous woman, *"Go, and sin no more" (John 8:11).*

Bible Evidence Of Curses

Chapter 5

Galatians 3:13
Christ hath redeemed us from the curse of the law, being made a curse for us: for it is written, Cursed is every one that hangeth on a tree:

Many people are living under a demonic attack and don't understand that they may be living under a curse. Most mainline churches don't even believe in "demon possession" let alone, living under a demonic curse.

After working for over 44 years in ministry, I have come in contact with good people who on the mission field, have come in contact with **"spirits of infirmity"** because some witch doctor has placed a curse on them. Please understand, if you are not taught that Satan is real and has great power, if you are not taught that even as a Christian you can be demonized, then you'll not have your guard up against such powers.

Just as Christians can have Spiritual Gifts so can people be empowered with unholy gifts. Satan can imitate all the Spiritual Gifts, what he can't do is imitate the "Fruit of the Spirit," love, joy, peace.

There have been missionaries who have come home because of a voodoo priest or some other cult who has placed them under a curse. Many Christians choose to ignore the fact that anyone who is ungodly can have that kind of power, so just by their ignorance they give power to the spirits of evil.

Demonic power can heal by simply removing the **"evil curse"** they have inflicted on a person. YES, heal! Not all healing is from God, or Divine Healing. All sickness is of the devil and therefore it is a spiritual thing and if all sickness comes from the devil then it is easy for him to remove that sickness. When I attended Indiana Christian University, in Dr. Lester Sumrall's class on Demonology, he told about a nurse who has been bound for 18 years, and after he prayed for her she was delivered. Her testimony was that she went home and from her naval she started to bleed, she then called her neighbor who was also a nurse, to come over. To their surprise, out of her naval came a hairy like worm almost 2 feet long. When it had all come out she could stand upright. She came back to the service the next night with this hairy worm like substance in a big jar of formaldehyde to show Dr. Sumrall and the people what had bound her for 18years.

Evidence

Galatians 3:13
Christ hath redeemed us from the curse of the law, being made a curse for us: for it is written, Cursed is every one that hangeth on a tree:

QUESTION: is if there is no such thing as a **"curse"** why does the Bible say that *"Christ has redeemed us from the curse of the law."* One of the main reasons that Christ died on the Cross was to remove the curse from man. The Bible gives a long list of curses that came on those who were disobedient to God's Laws. Moses, for example, told Israel that when they passed over Jordan, that they were to divide the tribes of Israel into two groups, six tribes were to stand on the top of Mount Gerizim and read the blessings upon the people that obey God's Laws. The other six tribes were to stand upon Mount Ebal to pronounce the curses on the disobedient. Upon coming into the Land, Joshua took the people to the place that Moses had spoken of and had the children of Israel pronounce the blessings and curses.

In the Book of Numbers three chapters are devoted to the struggle between Balak, the Moabite king, and Balaam, the local prophet. Balak tried to bribe Balaam to curse the Israelites who had arrived at the border of Moab: *"Behold, there is a people come out of Egypt, which covereth the face of the earth: come now, curse me them; peradventure I shall be able to overcome them, and drive them out" (Number 22:11).* Balaam had enough sense to know he shouldn't, *"I cannot go beyond the word of the LORD my God, to do less or more" (Number 22:18).*

Balak never gave up trying to get Balaam to curse Israel. Here is understanding of the ungodly who are under the control of demons, they never give up.

Three times Balaam's donkey balked and Balaam beat the donkey until at last God gave the donkey the power to speak, and he turned and spoke to the prophet. The donkey had more spiritual discerning than the prophet. The donkey saw an angel of the Lord which had a sword in his hand to kill Balaam. It was only when Balaam understood the wrath of God he had incurred that he turned back.

The New Testament shows us that we do have the power of life and death in our mouth, Jesus spoke to a tree which had no fruit, *"And Jesus answered and said unto it, No man eat fruit of thee hereafter for ever. And his disciples heard it" (Mark 11:14).* The next day Peter was amazed that the tree had withered from its roots up, *"And in the morning, as they passed by, they saw the fig tree dried up from the roots" (Mark 11:20).* There are those who will say, that was the Lord. But remember that while Jesus was on the earth He was in the flesh and He was subject to the laws of the flesh. Anything He did while in the flesh He said we can do. The Apostle Paul while preaching was confronted with a sorcerer, who by his power was trying to prevent Paul preaching the Gospel. Paul said, *"And now, behold, the hand of the Lord is upon thee, and thou shalt be blind, not seeing the sun for a season. And immediately there fell on him a mist and a darkness; and he went about seeking some to lead him by the hand" (Acts 13:11).* It should be noted that Elymas was only blinded for a time, so that Paul could preach and the people could hear without the power of the devil's interference.

Witchcraft Is Real

1 Samuel 15:23
For rebellion is as the sin of witchcraft, and stubbornness is as iniquity and idolatry. Because thou hast rejected the word of the LORD, he hath also rejected thee from being king.

Why would the Bible tells us that witchcraft is a sin if it does not exist? The Bible calls it a sin. It says:

- Witchcraft is sin
- Stubbornness is sin
- Idolatry is sin.

Look carefully at what this verse is saying. It says if we are *"rebellious"* which is being disobedient, or *"stubbornness,"* just how many "Christians" are obstinate, immovable, and stubborn? The Bible calls *"rebellion (disobedience), stubbornness, and idolatry"* a great sin and when we allow these sins into our life we are opening the door to demons and curses.

Here are some of the worldly practices that are forbidden by God's Word:

- **Enchantments** – Which is the practice of magical arts. (Exodus 7:11, 22; Exodus 8:7, 18; Leviticus 19:26; Isaiah 47:9, 12; Jeremiah. 27:9; Daniel 1:20).

- **Witchcraft** – The practice of dealing with evil spirits. (Exodus 22:18; Deuteronomy 18:10; 1 Samuel 15:23; 2 Chronicles 33:6; 2 Kings 9:22).

- **Sorcery** – Is the same thing as witchcraft. (Daniel 2:2; Malachi 3:5; Acts 8:9-11; Acts 13:6-8; Revelation 9:21; 18:23; 21:8; 22:15).

- **Sooth-saying** – Same as witchcraft. (Isaiah 2:6; Daniel 2:27; 4:7; 5:7, 11).

- **Divination** – The art of mystic in sight or fortune-telling (Numbers 22:7; 23:23; 2 Kings 17:17; 1 Samuel 6:2; Jer. 14:14; Acts 16:16).

- **Wizardly** – Same as witchcraft. A wizard is a male and a witch is a female who practices witchcraft. Both were to be destroyed in Israel (Exodus 22:18; Leviticus 19:31; 30:6, 27; Deuteronomy 18:11; 1 Samuel 28:1; 1 Chronicles 10:13).

- ➢ **Necromancy** – Divination by means of pretended communication with the dead (Deuteronomy 18:11; Isaiah 8:19; 1 Samuel 28:1; 1 Chronicles 10:13).

- ➢ **Magic** – Any pretended supernatural art or practice (Genesis 41:8, 24; Daniel 1:20; Daniel 2:2, 10, 27; Daniel 4:7, 9; Acts 19:19).

- ➢ **Charm** – To put a spell upon. Same as enchantment. (Deuteronomy 18:11; Isaiah 19:3 ;).

- ➢ **Prognostication** - To foretell by indication, omens, signs, etc. (Isaiah 47:13)

- ➢ **Observing Times** – Same as prognostication (Leviticus 19:26; Deuteronomy 18:10).

- ➢ **Astrology and Star Gazing** – Divination by the stars (Isaiah 47:13; Jeremiah 10:2; Daniel 1:23; 2:2, 10).

All the above practices were and are still carried on in connection with demons, or familiar spirits. All who forsake God and sought help from these demons were to be destroyed. The sad truth is that today many of the above are being brought into the church and because people and leaders are not on the spiritual level they should be they don't even know it.

> **King Saul had the position of anointing without having the anointing. It is so easy to allow a spirit of deception to come in our life. Pastors may have the position without having the anointing. Because you were once anointed, doesn't mean you are still anointed.**

> **Many times it is hard to tell the difference between someone who is cursed and anointed. It takes the Gift of Discernment, and even then at times it is hard to say.**

What Are Some Of the Signs Of Being Cursed?

Here is a list of five signs indicating that a person or family may be suffering from a curse:

1. **Mental or Emotional Breakdown.** Chronic depression usually has its source in some kind of occult activity – either the person's own involvement or that of an ancestor. While we know that not all depression can be traced back to a curse, it would be wise to consider it.

2. **Repeated or Chronic Sickness** – especially if it is hereditary. This is particularly true if physicians can't find any cause for the illness.

3. **Breakdown of Marriage and Family.** Satan knows if he can destroy the family he can destroy the Church.

4. **Continuing Financial Insufficiency.** When a person's education and salary indicates that they

should be able to get along, and they can't, something is wrong.

5. **Family History of Suicide.** While many families have a **"controlling spirit"** of one kind or the other, when a family has more than one suicide in it, it's a sign that a demon spirit of suicide has moved into that family.

The Church/Believers Are The Targets Of Satanic Covens

Why do you think that so many ministers are having family problems? Why is it that many times those who work the hardest in the kingdom of God are suffering so many attacks? All over America and around the world Satan is doing his best to target clergy marriages and churches and direct curses to destroy them in two ways:

1. **Creating Dissension in the Churches** – 1 Corinthians 14:33 *"For God is not the author of confusion, but of peace, as in all churches of the saints."* God has never caused a problem in one church, it is always the devil.

2. **Dividing Marriages through Lust and Adultery.** In addition to directing curses at the Church and families of their leaders, sometimes Satan will send a person into a Church to seduce the pastor or pastor's spouse. Every time a leader falls through lust and adultery the Church suffers for many years.

Again, I know that human weakness can count for many of our failings. But we also need to be aware of the reality of spiritual warfare and the need to pray for protection – and perhaps to be freed from the effects of a curse.

> **While a Christian cannot be possessed with demon spirits, they can be demonized. One of the things that we don't hear talked about is a "Causal demon" which can resist the power of God to heal or bless a person.**

Curses That Come On Us From Outside

Proverbs 26:2
As the bird by wandering, as the swallow by flying, so the curse causeless shall not come.

The New King James translation says, *"A curse without cause shall not alight."* In other words, we remain free from curses unless there is some reason for the curses to settle on us.

Curses come from two general categories:

1. **Curses that descend on us from past generations.** First of all I want to emphasize that we can be innocent of wrongdoing, yet be the victim of a curse if we have not protected ourselves and our families through prayer. The good news is that all curses can be broken by the power of God, through the blood of the Lamb.

These are called GENERATIONAL curses, their causes are:

a. **The family has been involved in the occult; especially if there have been witches or warlocks in the family tree.** When we consider that we have two parents, four grandparents, eight great-grandparents and sixteen great-great-grandparents, for a total of thirty in all, how many could guarantee that none of our thirty immediate ancestors was not involved in any form of idolatry or the occult?

b. **The family has been cursed by someone.**

c. **The family has been deeply involved in some kind of sinful activity.** Drugs, Sex, Idolatry, Etc.

These generational curses can have two effects. One, God's blessings may simply be blocked. The curse forms a barrier that needs to be broken so that God's blessings can flow upon the family.

Second, multiple disasters sometimes seem to target a family.

I heard about a lady missionary who had a mysterious fever and another missionary who scarcely knew her came to see her, and proceeded to ask her if she was of Cherokee descent, and when she said she was a missionary, she told her that God had shown her that she needed to have her bloodlines cleansed of the effect of witchcraft. After prayer the fever disappeared.

2. **Curses that come to us from some present cause.** Satan targets ministers and pastors who are about to come into another level of

anointing. It may be just as ordinary as a spirit of heaviness or depression; at other times, more seriously, by various kinds of illness; or, worse yet, by obsessive thoughts or desires tempting them toward divisive resentment or sexual promiscuity.

Inflected Curses

Chapter 6

We come to curses that people call down on themselves and do it sometimes unwittingly. We know that no one would willingly call down a curse on themselves but many times that is just what happens. This is a sad thing to even think about because it involves guilt and thoughts of the darkness.

Then there are times when people can get into such a state of mind that even though they know what they are doing, they do it anyway. What I do and how I do it is important.

There are four categories of sin that a person involves themselves in that can call down a curse on them:

1. Worship false gods.

We act like this would just happen to someone who lives in some backward country, but not so. Anytime you allow you mind and spirit to be taken over by thoughts and actions that you shouldn't, you are worshipping a false god. You may not think so, but everyone is worshipping something. It could be a job, house, or even family. Anything that we let come between us and our worship of the true and living God is worship of a false god. In fact it is the spirit of antichrist.

(Here is seed for thought)

Jeremiah 17:5-6

Thus saith the LORD; Cursed be the man that trusteth in man, and maketh flesh his arm, and whose heart departeth from the LORD. For he shall be like the heath in the desert, and shall not see when good cometh; but shall inhabit the parched places in the wilderness, in a salt land and not inhabited.

Legalism can be equated to worshipping false gods in that it encourages us to rely on our human abilities to accomplish what should be done only by the power of God.

Legalism causes good people to worship false gods. It causes Christians to be diverted from worshipping God and worship the law rather than the Law giver.

As believers we must not allow ourselves to rely on rules and concepts. People that do so pick up a spirit of self-glory rather than glorying in the leading of the Holy Spirit and Lordship of Jesus Christ.

Here are some things that one must watch out for:

Theology that is exalted above the written Word of God;
Psychology above discernment;
Programs above the leading of the Holy Spirit;
Reasoning above the walk of faith;
Laws above love.

2. **Disrespect for parents.**

   Satan knows that if he can destroy the family he can destroy the church. This is one of the signs of the second coming of the Lord and the end of the age, the break up of the family. In so many cases the children have been raised without any God-conscience and their parents have set such a bad example that they don't feel like they are worthy of honor. But the Bible doesn't say that they have to be worthy, it just says, ***"Honor thy father and mother."***

   With that said, parents are bringing curses upon their children by what they do and how they act. Much of the bondage that children are living under today is because parents have let the devil into their homes and the children pay the price.

3. **Oppression of people**

   There are people who want to have control over others. Not only is it wrong but according to the Bible, it's the spirit of Jezebel. Watch out for people who want to be in control and if they're not, then they won't do anything. There is a demon spirit of oppression, but what I'm talking about is not the person being oppressed but oppressing others.

> **A spirit of Jezebel is an Independent spirit, a controlling spirit. It has nothing to do with how a person dresses.**

4. Illicit or unnatural sex.

By the time we have seen and heard everything that is going on in our world today our mind has got to be cleansed, and the only way we can do it is to repent. We need to renounce what we have done and seen then turn from it.

Romans chapter one deals with the subject of illicit or unnatural sex, and the thing we must remember is that Paul was writing to the Church/Christians. We open ourselves up to live under a curse because we willingly open our minds and spirits to things that are unholy.

While a Christian cannot be demon possessed, the next best thing for Satan is to have them live under bondage through a curse, and many times we pass that curse on to our family. Remember that the Bible says, *"Thou shalt not bow down thyself unto them, nor serve them: for I the LORD thy God am a jealous God, visiting the iniquity of the fathers upon the children unto the third and fourth generation of them that hate me, And shewing mercy unto thousands of them that love me and keep my commandments" (Deuteronomy 5:-10).*

We are deeply affected by other people's feelings (positive or negative) towards us – their love, hate or apathy that is only human. When a child is told, **"they are stupid and will never amount to anything",** something deep down on the inside of the child believes it and their life is cursed. Feelings of low self-esteem or worthlessness are passed on from parents to the child and will stay in until someone wants deliverance.

> **Negative words cut like a knife and remain for a lifetime. Only the blood of Jesus can remove the negative things from our life.**

Self-Imposed Curses

It is always easier to avoid things that cause us pain. How many times have you said, **"I'm not going to try that again"** or when things go wrong they groan, **"I wish I was dead"**? These are self-imposed curses.

> **Some people don't have to have anyone else place a curse on them, they are their worst enemy, or their mouth is.**

Personal Deliverance Ministry Checklist

> Note: The following questionnaire should be filled out before you even try to bring deliverance in a person's life.

1 Thess. 5:23
And the very God of peace sanctify you wholly; and I pray God your whole spirit and soul and body be preserved blameless unto the coming of our Lord Jesus Christ.

Name: _____

Date: _____

Address: _____

City _____ **State** ____ **Zip** _____

Church they attend: _____

Pastor's Name _____

Ancestral Information

Father's Side   **Mother's Side**

Great Grandfather Name: _____ **Great Grandfather Name:** _____

Any background information or involvements

_____ _____
_____ _____

Great Grandmother	Great Grandmother
Name: _____	Name: _____

Any background information/involvements

_____   _____
_____   _____

Grandfather	Grandfather
Name: _____	Name: _____

Background information/involvements

_____   _____
_____   _____

Father	Father
Name: _____	Name: _____

Background/Involvements

_____   _____
_____   _____

Mother	Mother
Name: _____	Name: _____

Background/Involvement

_____   _____
_____   _____

<u>Family History</u>
(Please check all that apply)

Parents, grandparents involved in:

1. Church _____

2. Occultic Practice: _____
3. Cultic groups: _____

4. Idol worship: _____

Recurring problems in the family line:

( ) adulterous affairs

( ) homosexuality/lesbianism

( ) mental illness

( ) suicides, violent tendencies

( ) barrenness, tendency to miscarry or related female problems

( ) addictive problems (alcohol, drugs)

( ) sickness / ailments

    ___ Tuberculosis
    ___ Diabetes
    ___ Cancer
    ___ Heart Disease
    ___ Asthma
    ___ Others (specify) _____

Do you know of any curses pronounced on the family?
_____
_____

Personal History

Spiritual involvements/experiences:

a. Occult
   ___ astrology   ___ crystal ball
   ___ Mind control   ___ horoscope
   ___ Acupressure   ___ martial arts
   ___ palm reading   ___ acupuncture
   ___ Witchcraft   ___ Ouji Board
   ___ Fortune telling   ___ other: _____

b. Cults/ name them:
   _____

c. Other experiences and involvements
   _____

d. Emotions / things that are difficult to control:

   ___Frustration   ___Pride   ___Rebellion
   ___Loneliness   ___Anger   ___Jealousy
   ___Hatred   ___Feelings of worthlessness
   ___Depression   ___Self-pity ___Bitterness
   ___Rejection   ___Unforgiveness
   ___Anxiety   ___Envy
   ___Fear of losing mind   ___ Suicidal tendency
   ___Others (specify) _____

e. Addiction or unusual cravings for
   ___Sweets   ___Drugs   ___Smoking
   ___Alcohol   ___Food   ___Sleep
   ___Rock Music
   ___Others (specify) _____

f. Other physical problems

   ____Recurring sickness or ailments (Specify)
   _____
   _____

___Recurring nightmares or disturbances
___Physically beaten ___Sexual molested

g. **Sexual problems**

___Masturbation
___Heavy petting and pre-marital sex
___Gay/lesbian relationships
___Pornography
___Incest
___sexually abused or has sexually abused others
___Others (specify) _____

h. **Bad Habits**

___Lying   ___Slandering
___Stealing   ___Peeping
___Gambling
___Others (specify) _____

Generational Curses

Chapter 7

Deuteronomy 30:19
I call heaven and earth to record this day against you, that I have set before you life and death, blessing and cursing: therefore choose life, that both thou and thou seed may live.

When a person chooses to walk in obedience to God, they are assured of the blessings of God upon their life; and these blessings will be passed down to their children and their children's children. Stop and think, if your children are blessed by your obedience then when you choose to ignore God's commandments, or openly rebel against God's laws, you bring a curse upon your children. Furthermore, the curse will be passed down to your descendants.

Exodus 20:4-6
Thou shalt not make unto thee any graven image, or any likeness of any thing that is in heaven above, or that is in the earth beneath, or that is in the water under the earth: Thou shalt not bow down thyself to them, nor serve them: for I the Lord thy God am a jealous God, visiting the iniquity of the fathers upon the children unto the third and fourth generation of them that hate me; And shewing mercy unto thousands of them that love me, and keep my commandments.

When God met with Moses on Mt. Sinai and gave him the Ten Commandments, God forbid idolatry under penalty of a curse that would pass down *"unto the third and the fourth generation" (Exodus 34:7).* Suppose a person did commit the sin of idolatry, which includes anything of the occult, his seed would come under the curse of that one man's iniquity.

Stop and think, each one of us have thirty ancestors (Parents, grandparents, etc.) from which curses have possibly come. If we look at this question in the light of parents, grandparents, great grandparents, great-great grandparents we can see how we could be suffering under some sort of curse due to ancestral sins.

The question is how can we know what particular idolatries our fore parents have committed? If we don't know what can we do? You need to find someone who knows the power of the Holy Spirit, for many times ancestral curses can be revealed by a *"word of knowledge."*

Ancestral curses are most often determined by the ill effects. Deuteronomy 28 lists several effects of curses that can be paraphrased as follows:

1. Poverty or perpetual financial insufficiency.
2. Barrenness and impotency together with miscarriages and related female complication.
3. Projects and plans always seem to meet with disaster.
4. Untimely and unnatural deaths.
5. Sickness and diseases; especially chronic and hereditary diseases.
6. Going from one crisis to another. Life traumas.
7. Mental and emotional breakdown.
8. Breakdown of family relationship, including divorce.

9. Unable to hear God's voice and know His will for your life.
10. Unable to understand God's Word and concentration in prayer, devoid of spiritual gifts.

If throughout the Old Testament Israel witnessed the operation of generational curses then we should understand that in the New Testament they are still in effect. As we have already noted, they devised a proverb to describe the effects of a father's sin being passed down. They said, *"The fathers have eaten sour grapes, and the children's teeth are set on edge"* **(Ezekiel 18:2).** The GOOD NEWS is that God declared that the time would come when this proverb would no longer be appropriate because there would come a NEW COVENANT. Under the New Covenant God would write His laws in their heart and every man be responsible for their own sins.

Jeremiah 31:29-33
In those days they shall say no more, The fathers have eaten a sour grape, and the children's teeth are set on edge. But every one shall die for his own iniquity: every man that eateth the sour grape, his teeth shall be set on edge. Behold, the days come, saith the Lord, that I will make a new covenant with the house of Israel, and with the house of Judah: Not according to the covenant that I made with their fathers in the day that I took them by the hand to bring them out of the land of Egypt; which my covenant they brake, although I was an husband unto them, saith the Lord: But this shall be the covenant that I will make with the house of Israel; After those days, saith the Lord, I will put my law in their inward parts, and write it in their hearts; and will be their God, and they shall be my people.

Ezekiel 18:1-4

The word of the Lord came unto me again, saying, What mean ye, that ye use this proverb concerning the land of Israel, saying, The fathers have eaten sour grapes, and the children's teeth are set on edge? As I live, saith the Lord God, ye shall not have occasion any more to use this proverb in Israel. Behold, all souls are mine; as the soul of the father, so also the soul of the son is mine: the soul that sinneth, it shall die.

This Covenant is the covenant of Grace that is provided through the shedding of His blood on the Cross of Calvary.

GRACE DOES NOT MEAN THAT A CURSE CAN NO LONGER BE PASSED DOWN THROUGH THE GENERATIONS. Grace means that Jesus paid the price for my deliverance through His substitutionary death, thus providing a remedy for my sins.

Galatians 3:13
Christ hath redeemed us from the curse of the law, being made a curse for us: for it is written, Cursed is every one that hangeth on a tree:

Here is the wisdom of the ages, if we find evidence of a generational curse operating in their life they should appropriate the provision that Christ made at Calvary. The Bible teaches us that we must confess our sins and the sins (known and unknown) of their forefathers. Don't forget that the effects of curses are merely the works of the devil which Jesus Christ has come to and did destroy. *"He that committed sin is of the devil; for the devil sinneth from the beginning. For this purpose the Son of God was manifested, that He might destroy the works of the devil" (1 John 3:8).* What this means for you and I is that the demons that perpetuate curses can now be driven out in the Name and by the Blood of Jesus Christ.

One of the greatest problems in people getting delivered from these generational curses is that they don't want to come clean with themselves or to acknowledge that their foreparents had anything wrong in their life.

Remember what Nehemiah did when he heard about the problems that were plaguing Israel. He not only repented of his sins but those of his father's house. This should give us insight to what we need to do and how we need to pray.

Nehemiah 1:6
Let thine ear now be attentive, and thine eyes open, that thou mayest hear the prayer of thy servant, which I pray before thee now, day and night, for the children of Israel thy servants, <u>and confess the sins of the children of Israel, which we have sinned</u> against thee: both I and my father's house have sinned.

Here are the facts, it's not that God is holding our sins over our children's head, it's that when we sin we open a door for demon spirits, and those spirits will not leave by themselves, they must be cast out. Satan NEVER gives up ground, we must fight and take it back by force.

Curses That We Bring On Ourselves

Many of God's people are struggling against adversities and evil in their lives without understanding that their problems are due to curses. Curses come in because someone OPENED the DOOR. And it doesn't have to be a big door, it can be the size of a speck.

Deuteronomy 27:26
Cursed be he that confirmeth not all the words of this law to do them. And all the people shall say, Amen.

(NIV) Deuteronomy 27:26
Cursed is the man who does not uphold the words of this law by carrying them out.

Sin is disobedience to God's laws. In God's sight, partial obedience is still disobedience. King Saul was told by God to totally destroy all the Amalekites, but Saul brought back some of the best things, sheep, oxen, and the fat calves and lambs "to offer up to God." He even spared the king. Isn't it wonderful how we can cover up our disobedience with something religious! Saul was not to spare a man, woman, child or livestock. Everything pertaining to the Amalakites was to be destroyed.

Saul's partial obedience was judged to be rebellion – EVEN THE SIN OF WITCHCRAFT.
1 Samuel 15:23
For rebellion is as the sin of witchcraft, and stubbornness is as iniquity and idolatry. Because thou hast rejected the word of the Lord, he hath also rejected thee from being king.

Ask yourself the question, have you disobeyed God's laws? Have you refused to do what He told you to do? I'm talking about just while you've been "a Christian?" If your answer is yes, you probably have cause to think that something may be going on in Satan's workshop to bring a curse upon you or your family.

How To Pray For Removal Of Curses

If you have been cursed or even think you have, you can be freed by:

1. Clearing your spirit before God
2. Asking forgiveness of anyone that you feel you need to.
3. Then pray this prayer:
   "In the Name of Jesus Christ and by the power of the Holy Spirit, I am set free from the false spirits and curse of _____ and declare it null and void.

If you have brought a curse upon yourself by something that you may have said or done pray this prayer:

1. I repent of _____
2. I break the power of Satan in the Name of Jesus Christ over my life. I break this curse _____ and declare it null and void, no longer will it be able to have control of my life or have any influence over me.

When praying these prayers if you discern a presence of any demon spirits, command them to leave and not come back in the Name of Jesus.

First Bind The Strong Man

Chapter 8

Matthew 12:29
Or else how can one enter into a strong man's house, and spoil his goods, except he first bind the strong man? and then he will spoil his house.

I heard about a man, let's call him Bob, who shortly after parking in front of the office, a well-dressed businessman backed into his car, causing no more than a slight scratch on his fender. Bob told the man to forget the incident, but the business man insisted on doing something. He asked Bob for his address and promised to send him two tickets to a play. Two weeks later, the tickets arrived, designating their seats and time. Along with the tickets came a box of candy and a gift certificate for dinner at a very plush restaurant near the Performing Arts Center. An entire night's entertainment was being provided in exchange for a mere scuff on Bob's car. He and his wife were thrilled to say the least!

What a night it was until Bob and his wife arrived home. As they pulled into the driveway something felt wrong. Then, when they opened the door to the house, both Bob and his wife began to sob. They had been duped- unsuspecting victims of a slick thief who had planned the whole thing. Their house was empty, everything was gone, while they were out on the town the thieves had packed everything they owned into a moving van and hauled it away. They were taken advantage of because they didn't understand the schemes of the enemy.

Each and every one of us have been robbed in some way by Satan, the strong man, who has come *"to steal, to kill and to destroy" (John 10:10).* In Matthew 12:29 Jesus gave us understanding of what we need to do and the first thing: *"First bind the strong man,"* and then recover stolen goods. According to 2 Corinthians 2:11, *"Lest Satan should get an advantage of us: for we are not ignorant of his devices"* – that is, his plots or strategies to ruin our spiritual lives and sabotage our destinies.

Jesus said that we are to *"first bind the strong man that we might recover all the goods he has stolen."* What has the enemy stolen from you today? Last week? Last month? Last year? How about in your lifetime? What is due you that you must recover by faith through prayer and the authority of God's Word?

What in your life has "old slick, the devil" come to steal?

- He has come *"to steal":* You used to have it, but now it is gone. He stole it from you. It no longer exists in your life.

- He comes *"to kill":* It was alive and flourishing and bearing fruit, but now it's dead.

- He comes *"to destroy":* There was something in your life that could have been very powerful, but the enemy stopped it, destroyed it, hindered it, and crippled it.

The Bible teaches that what we lost in Adam we have gained back in Christ. Only you know where you feel ripped off, only you know what *"the strong man"* has stolen from you. What I know is that whatever you have lost, part of your Kingdom inheritance is to rightly reclaim all that you have lost.

2 Timothy 2:26
And that they may recover themselves out of the snare of the devil, who are taken captive by him at his will.

Where has the devil ensnared, trapped you, even to the point that you have cooperated with him to do his will? We all must admit that there have been times when like Bob, we have played right into the hands of the thief, and because of his lies we have even cooperated with him to some extent, and by doing so, helped him steal from us. Therefore, we need help in recovering whatever he has deceptively taken from us.

Recover All

1 Samuel 30:18
And David recovered all that the Amalekites had carried away: and David rescued his two wives.

1 Samuel 30:19
And there was nothing lacking to them, neither small nor great, neither sons nor daughters, neither spoil, nor any thing that they had taken to them: David recovered all.

We need to believe that, like David of old, we can recover all and nothing will be lacking, either small or great. Let's pray that the Holy Spirit would begin to stir our hearts with faith to recall even the small and seemingly insignificant things that have been robbed from us – things that according to God's Word, are important because without them we cannot completely fulfill the destiny God has for us.

> **Satan is the MASTER THIEF. He steals from us and makes us believe that we can never recover, but he is a liar, and the father of liars.**

Total Deliverance

Jesus teaches us that in order to recover all; we first must bind the strong man before we can plunder his goods:

Matthew 12:29
Or else how can one enter into a strong man's house, and spoil his goods, except he first bind the strong man? and then he will spoil his house.

Before we get in Matthew 12:29, we need to look at the context in which it is found, in Matthew 11:28-30 Jesus made a promise for all who would come to him, that He would give rest. To have that rest you must be delivered from everything that would bind you, including all curses.

Matthew 11:28-30
Come unto me, all ye that labour and are heavy laden, and I will give you rest. ^{29} Take my yoke upon you, and learn of me; for I am meek and lowly in heart: and ye shall find rest unto your souls. ^{30} For my yoke is easy, and my burden is light.

It seems to me that many Christians don't understand what they have in Christ, and because of their lack of understanding they are destroyed. Hosea, the prophet, warned God's people about their lack of knowledge and because of their lack of knowledge their rejection of God's laws.

Hosea 4:6
My people are destroyed for lack of knowledge: because thou hast rejected knowledge, I will also reject thee, that thou shalt be no priest to me: seeing thou hast forgotten the law of thy God, I will also forget thy children.

God didn't bring Israel out of Egypt's bondage just to get them out of Egypt or out of the control of Pharaoh. God brought them out so that they could have a relationship with Him. Short of that they might as well be in Egypt.
God doesn't deliver a person out of bondage of (sin, sickness, curses) anything just to be delivering them; He wants a relationship with them.

One of the big hindrances to many Christians is LEGALISM. In the first part of Matthew chapter 12, Jesus explained how belief in Him and His doctrine will deliver people from the yoke of man-made religious traditions. Please note what Jesus did; He not only maintained His personal integrity, but the integrity of His ministry. At the same time He exposed the inadequacy of the religious system of His time and its lack of purpose in relationship with God. They were worshipping a system of worship. This is one of the BIGGEST CURSES that we deal with.

During the temptation in the wilderness and throughout His ministry, Jesus was in conflict with satanic influences. He came in contact with the powers of Satan who was always around where He was. Why is it that we can talk about the "ANOINTING OF THE SPIRIT" and at the same time not be aware that Satan knows where and what is going on around us. It ought not surprise us that Satan tries us, because if he tried Jesus, Peter, James, John, and Paul, we should understand he will try us also.

> **This is part of the "lack of knowledge" that Hosea spoke about.**

Jesus The Deliverer

Jesus came to bring freedom from internal and external bondages – past, present, and future bondages. He died so that we can *"have life, and that they (we) might have it more abundantly" (John 10:10).*

In Matthew 12:29 *"Or else how can one enter into a strong man's house, and spoil his goods, except he first bind the strong man? and then he will spoil his house."* Jesus is underscoring His argument of Matthew 12:28 *"But if I cast out devils by the Spirit of God, then the kingdom of God is come unto you."* He compares Satan to the master of the house and the demon-possessed to household articles. Jesus bases His argument upon the common beliefs that Satan is a powerful spirit and that the spirits can only be cast by stronger spirits. Jesus overcomes and defeats Satan through the power of the kingdom of God and by the power of the Holy Spirit.

> **Once again, God didn't bring Israel out of bondage just to be bringing them out. He brought them out so that they could have relationship with Him. NO ONE WILL EVER be set free just to be set free! The plan and purpose of God in everything He does is RELATIONSHIP.**

> **In pagan minds, "BIND" was used to describe the power exercised over someone by either a sorcerer, a god or a spirit. Releasing from that spirit was called "loosing," setting that person free and removing the power that held them bound.**
> **Matthew 18:18**
> *Verily I say unto you, Whatsoever ye shall bind on earth shall be bound in heaven: and whatsoever ye shall loose on earth shall be loosed in heaven.*

1 Peter 5:8-9
Be sober, be vigilant; because your adversary the devil, as a roaring lion, walketh about, seeking whom he may devour: ⁹ Whom resist stedfast in the faith, knowing that the same afflictions are accomplished in your brethren that are in the world.

What is so hard to understand about the word *"resist?"* It means to stand against – that is, to firmly plant your feet so that you can not be moved. You have not *"resisted steadfastly"* while you are listening to what he has to say about anything. Remember, Satan is a liar.

Ephesians 4:27
Neither give place to the devil.

How do we *"give place to the devil?"* By letting what he is saying and doing bring fear to our spirit. As believers we should not give place either by word or deed. According to this Scripture Satan doesn't have a place until we give it to him.

Proverbs 5:22
His own iniquities shall take the wicked himself, and he shall be holden with the cords of his sins.

It's our own sins that we will be judged for. Satan cannot make us sin, we chose whom we serve. We give Satan power over us, and if it is something we GIVE then we can take it away from him.

John 8:36
If the Son therefore shall make you free, ye shall be free indeed.

What does *"free indeed"* mean? Does it mean for just awhile? Or does it mean that it will come back? NO! When we are set free, we are *"free indeed."*

2 Timothy 2:25-26
In meekness instructing those that oppose themselves; if God peradventure will give them repentance to the acknowledging of the truth; [26] *And that they may recover themselves out of the snare of the devil, who are taken captive by him at his will.*

We are to approach those who are wrong with the spirit of meekness. Here is where so many go wrong, they try to deal with people in the wrong with the same wrong spirit, it just doesn't work. By arguing and fighting with them we become guilty of the same wrong.

People who are always controversial and argumentative, critical and gossiping may not like to think that they are ensnared by the devil, but the Bible is clear, they are. Note what the above verse says, **"Snared of the devil, who are taken captive by him at his will."** Satan takes them at his will because of how they live or react.

John 12:31
Now is the judgment of this world: now shall the prince of this world be cast out.

While Satan may be a ruler today, according to Revelation, the day will come when he is cast down. He is already defeated to those who know the power of the Blood of Jesus and are walking in FAITH.

John 14:30
Hereafter I will not talk much with you: for the prince of this world cometh, and hath nothing in me.

Although Satan, the prince of this world, was unable to defeat Jesus in the Wilderness Temptation, he is so arrogant that he will continue to try. Because Jesus is sinless Satan can not have any power over Him.

John 16:11
Of judgment, because the prince of this world is judged.

At the cross Satan was judged and because of the sinless life of our Lord Jesus Christ, God declares us righteous and delivers us from the judgment of our sins.

1 John 5:19
And we know that we are of God, and the whole world lieth in wickedness.

Unless a person comes to Christ and gives their heart and soul to Him they have no choice but to serve the devil. There is no middle ground, either they are saved and on their way to heaven or they are living in sin and on their way to hell.

2 Corinthians 4:4
In whom the god of this world hath blinded the minds of them which believe not, lest the light of the glorious gospel of Christ, who is the image of God, should shine unto them.

Satan is the god of this world and he has blinded those who are not saved. How does he do it, through the lust for money, power, and pleasure etc...

Ephesians 2:2
Wherein in time past ye walked according to the course of this world, according to the prince of the power of the air, the spirit that now worketh in the children of disobedience:

Paul said that was our condition in *"time past."* And note it is the spirit of disobedience.

Exposing The Deeds Of Darkness

Chapter 9

Ephesians 5:11
And have no fellowship with the unfruitful works of darkness, but rather reprove them.

> **Satan's number one tool to destroy churches is <u>a spirit of faultfinding.</u> The spirit of faultfinding has almost been elevated to a ministry.**

Why is it that so called "Spirit Filled" people get their eyes off the perfections of the Lord Jesus Christ and onto the **imperfection of one another?** When they do, they become the tool of Satan to bring trouble into the Body of Christ. This faultfinding spirit many times will masquerade as the **spirit of discernment**, and the problem is that everyone will be caught up in it at sometime in their life.

Some think it's a great thing if they can find fault in the Pastor or a Church member, they take it as a sign of being **spiritual,** but all it does is show that they have a judgmental spirit. After all, if you have not personally talked to the individual of whom you are critical, how do you know you are not fulfilling the role of *"the accuser of the brethren?"* The Bible says in John 7:51 *"Doth our law judge any man, before it hear him, and know what he doeth?"* So, we must watch out that this spirit doesn't have a place in our heart.

> **WARNING! Many demonic spirits will put on Religious clothing to hide its true nature.**

James 1:26
If any man among you seem to be religious, and bridleth not his tongue, but deceiveth his own heart, this man's religion is vain.

The Next question is, how does one protect ones self from the criticism of ungodly tongues? The fact is, that people are going to talk, but godly people will not become *"the accuser of the brethren" (Revelation 12:10)* for that is the work of Satan. The Bible is clear how godly people handle things, *Doth our law judge any man, before it hear him, and know what he doeth" (John 7:51).* The Bible also says, *"neither give place to the devil" (Ephesians 4:27)* and when we let go with our tongue we have just given place to the devil. I hear people say, "I meant well" and that's a lie, when we let our tongue go we really are speaking from the *"abundance of the heart"*

Luke 6:45
A good man out of the good treasure of his heart bringeth forth that which is good; and an evil man out of the evil treasure of his heart bringeth forth that which is evil: for of the abundance of the heart his mouth speaketh.

If you work for God people will talk, if you don't people will still talk, GET OVER IT. If it's any comfort, Jesus said, *"to beware when all men speak well of us"* One of Satan's greatest tools to distract God's people with is *"the scourge of the tongue" (Job 5:21).*

Luke 6:26
Woe unto you, when all men shall speak well of you! for so did their fathers to the false prophets.

WHY deal with the tongue? It is a tool of Satan!!!! When Satan is successful, everyone involved will lose and will suffer because of a TONGUE ATTACK.

WARNING !!!! For everyone who takes a hammer and chisel and tries to make the man or woman of God a hero, there is someone else with a hammer and spikes ready to crucify them.

PLEASE don't forget that Christians are not superman. Bullets (words) don't bounce off their chest, they do damage to them just like anyone else. If our words offend God, how much more difficult is it for His servants to remain aloof from the conflict that sin causes.

Proverbs 6:16-19
These six things doth the LORD hate: yea, seven are an abomination unto him: A proud look, a lying tongue, and hands that shed innocent blood, An heart that deviseth wicked imaginations, feet that be swift in running to mischief, A false witness that speaketh lies, and he that soweth discord among brethren.

Here is one of the most important things that I will ever write:
Anytime a person is acting out of an embittered spirit, they are not trying to help you, but destroy you.

Christians who have allowed themselves to be used of the devil have done more damage to the body of Christ than all the "outsiders" together. While a Christian cannot be demon possessed they can be demonized, in other words Satan can control them at times.

1 Timothy 4:1-3
Now the Spirit speaketh expressly, that in the latter times some shall depart from the faith, giving heed to seducing spirits, and doctrines of devils; ²Speaking lies in hypocrisy; having their conscience seared with a hot iron; ³Forbidding to marry, and commanding to abstain from meats, which God hath created to be received with thanksgiving of them which believe and know the truth.

It is very interesting that in the last days demon spirits will teach *(doctrines of devils)* and they will attack the family *(forbidding to marry)*.

Other Deadly "Little" Demons

1. Filthy thoughts

Matthew 5:27-30
Ye have heard that it was said by them of old time, Thou shalt not commit adultery: ²⁸But I say unto you, That whosoever looketh on a woman to lust after her hath committed adultery with her already in his heart. ²⁹And if thy right eye offend thee, pluck it out, and cast it from thee: for it is profitable for thee that one of thy members should perish, and not that thy whole body should be cast into hell. ³⁰And if thy right hand offend thee, cut if

off, and cast it from thee: for it is profitable for thee that one of thy members should perish, and not that thy whole body should be cast into hell.

James 1:14-15
But every man is tempted, when he is drawn away of his own lust, and enticed. ¹⁵Then when lust hath conceived, it bringeth forth sin: and sin, when it is finished, bringeth forth death.

2. Lying spirits

Genesis 3:3-4
But of the fruit of the tree which is in the midst of the garden, God hath said, Ye shall not eat of it, neither shall ye touch it, lest ye die. ⁴And the serpent said unto the woman, Ye shall not surely die:

1 Kings 13:18-19
He said unto him, I am a prophet also as thou art; and an angel spake unto me by the word of the LORD, saying, Bring him back with thee into thine house, that he may eat bread and drink water. But he lied unto him. ¹⁹So he went back with him, and did eat bread in his house, and drank water.

Acts 5:1-3
But a certain man named Ananias, with Sapphira his wife, sold a possession, ²And kept back part of the price, his wife also being privy to it, and brought a certain part, and laid it at the apostles' feet. ³But Peter said, Ananias, why hath Satan filled thine heart to lie to the Holy Ghost, and to keep back part of the price of the land?

3. **Jealousy**

    Proverbs 6:34
    For jealousy is the rage of a man: therefore he will not spare in the day of vengeance.

    Songs of Solomon 8:6
    Set me as a seal upon thine heart, as a seal upon thine arm: for love is strong as death; jealousy is cruel as the grave: the coals thereof are coals of fire, which hath a most vehement flame.

4. **Perverse spirit (stubbornness, Rebellious)**

    1 Samuel 15:23
    For rebellion is as the sin of witchcraft, and stubbornness is as iniquity and idolatry. Because thou hast rejected the word of the LORD, he hath also rejected thee from being king.

5. **Unforgiveness**

    Mark 11:25
    And when ye stand praying, forgive, if ye have ought against any: that your Father also which is in heaven may forgive you your trespasses.

    Luke 7:4
    And when they came to Jesus, they besought him instantly, saying, That he was worthy for whom he should do this:

Ephesians 4:32
And be ye kind one to another, tenderhearted, forgiving one another, even as God for Christ's sake hath forgiven you.

Colossians 3:13
Forbearing one another, and forgiving one another, if any man have a quarrel against any: even as Christ forgave you, so also do ye.

6. **Fear**

    Job 3:25
    For the thing which I greatly feared is come upon me, and that which I was afraid of is come unto me.

    2 Timothy 1:7
    For God hath not given us the spirit of fear; but of power, and of love, and of a sound mind.

7. **Hateful spirit**

    Titus 3:3
    For we ourselves also were sometimes foolish, disobedient, deceived, serving divers lusts and pleasures, living in malice and envy, hateful, and hating one another.

8. **Evil Imagination**

    Romans 1:21
    Because that, when they knew God, they glorified him not as God, neither were thankful; but became vain in their imaginations, and their foolish heart was darkened.

9. Covetousness

>Exodus 20:17
>Thou shalt not covet thy neighbour's house, thou shalt not covet thy neighbour's wife, nor his manservant, nor his maidservant, nor his ox, nor his ass, nor any thing that is thy neighbour's.

>Luke 12:15
>And he said unto them, Take heed, and beware of covetousness: for a man's life consisteth not in the abundance of the things which he possesseth.

>Colossians 3:5
>Mortify therefore your members which are upon the earth; fornication, uncleanness, inordinate affection, evil concupiscence, and covetousness, which is idolatry:

10. Worry

>Matthew 6:25-34
>Therefore I say unto you, Take no thought for your life, what ye shall eat, or what ye shall drink; nor yet for your body, what ye shall put on. Is not the life more than meat, and the body than raiment? [26]Behold the fowls of the air: for they sow not, neither do they reap, nor gather into barns; yet your heavenly Father feedeth them. Are ye not much better than they? [27]Which of you by taking thought can add one cubit unto his stature? [28]And why take ye thought for raiment? Consider the lilies of the field, how they grow; they toil not, neither do they spin: [29]And yet I say unto you, That even Solomon in all his glory was not

arrayed like one of these. ³⁰Wherefore, if God so clothe the grass of the field, which to day is, and to morrow is cast into the oven, shall he not much more clothe you, O ye of little faith? ³¹Therefore take no thought, saying, What shall we eat? or, What shall we drink? or, Wherewithal shall we be clothed? ³²(For after all these things do the Gentiles seek:) for your heavenly Father knoweth that ye have need of all these things. ³³But seek ye first the kingdom of God, and his righteousness; and all these things shall be added unto you. ³⁴Take therefore no thought for the morrow: for the morrow shall take thought for the things of itself. Sufficient unto the day is the evil thereof.

Philippians 4:4-8
Rejoice in the Lord alway: and again I say, Rejoice. ⁵Let your moderation be known unto all men. The Lord is at hand. ⁶Be careful for nothing; but in every thing by prayer and supplication with thanksgiving let your requests be made known unto God. ⁷And the peace of God, which passeth all understanding, shall keep your hearts and minds through Christ Jesus. ⁸Finally, brethren, whatsoever things are true, whatsoever things are honest, whatsoever things are just, whatsoever things are pure, whatsoever things are lovely, whatsoever things are of good report; if there be any virtue, and if there be any praise, think on these things.

11. Religious spirit

Matthew 6:16
Moreover when ye fast, be not, as the hypocrites, of a sad countenance: for they disfigure their

faces, that they may appear unto men to fast. Verily I say unto you, They have their reward.

Matthew 12:2
But when the Pharisees saw it, they said unto him, Behold, thy disciples do that which is not lawful to do upon the sabbath day.

Matthew 23:4
For they bind heavy burdens and grievous to be borne, and lay them on men's shoulders; but they themselves will not move them with one of their fingers.

12. Worldly spirit

Romans 12:1-2
I beseech you therefore, brethren, by the mercies of God, that ye present your bodies a living sacrifice, holy, acceptable unto God, which is your reasonable service. ²And be not conformed to this world: but be ye transformed by the renewing of your mind, that ye may prove what is that good, and acceptable, and perfect, will of God.

1) Pride

Proverbs 16:18
Pride goeth before destruction, and an haughty spirit before a fall.

1 Peter 3:3
Whose adorning let it not be that outward adorning of plaiting the hair, and of wearing of gold, or of putting on of apparel;

1 John 2:15-16
Love not the world, neither the things that are in the world. If any man love the world, the love of the Father is not in him. [16]For all that is in the world, the lust of the flesh, and the lust of the eyes, and the pride of life, is not of the Father, but is of the world.

2) Uncleanness

2 Corinthians 7:11
For behold this selfsame thing, that ye sorrowed after a godly sort, what carefulness it wrought in you, yea, what clearing of yourselves, yea, what indignation, yea, what fear, yea, what vehement desire, yea, what zeal, yea, what revenge! In all things ye have approved yourselves to be clear in this matter.

James 1:21
Wherefore lay apart all filthiness and superfluity of naughtiness, and receive with meekness the engrafted word, which is able to save your souls.

3) Modesty

1 Corinthians 11:5-15
But every woman that prayeth or prophesieth with her head uncovered dishonoureth her head: for that is even all one as if she were shaven. [6]For if the woman be not covered, let her also be shorn: but if it be a shame for a woman to be shorn or shaven, let her be covered. [7]For a man indeed ought not to cover

his head, forasmuch as he is the image and glory of God: but the woman is the glory of the man. ⁸For the man is not of the woman; but the woman of the man. ⁹Neither was the man created for the woman; but the woman for the man. ¹⁰For this cause ought the woman to have power on her head because of the angels. ¹¹Nevertheless neither is the man without the woman, neither the woman without the man, in the Lord. ¹²For as the woman is of the man, even so is the man also by the woman; but all things of God. ¹³Judge in yourselves: is it comely that a woman pray unto God uncovered? ¹⁴Doth not even nature itself teach you, that, if a man have long hair, it is a shame unto him? ¹⁵But if a woman have long hair, it is a glory to her: for her hair is given her for a covering.

13. **Idolatry** – This is the first sin that brings a curse. God looks upon Idolatry as spiritual adultery. The reason that God gives for extending a curse to the third and fourth generation is: *"I the Lord thy God am a JEALOUS God" (Ex. 20:5).*

Deuteronomy 7:25-26
*The graven images of their gods shall ye burn with fire: thou shalt not desire the silver or gold that is on them, nor take it unto thee, lest thou be snared therein: for it is an abomination to the L*ORD *thy God. ²⁶Neither shalt thou bring an abomination into thine house, lest thou be a cursed thing like it: but thou shalt utterly detest it, and thou shalt utterly abhor it; for it is a cursed thing.*

Look At How Satan Works

1. **Obsession** – "To fill the mind of; keep the attention of; haunt; influence of a feeling, idea, or impulse that a person cannot escape."

2. **Oppression** – "A being oppressed or burdened: cruel or unjust treatment: a heavy, weary feeling."

3. **Possession** – "To have control of; influence strongly; maintain; keep. Domination by a particular feeling, or idea. Controlled by an emotion or as if by an evil spirit; crazed; mad."

Demon Spirits Cause Sickness And Disease

Chapter 10

Job 2:7
So went Satan forth from the presence of the LORD, and smote Job with sore boils from the sole of his foot unto his crown.

Throughout the Bible we have infallible proof that evil spirits or demons bring sickness and disease upon the human body. Stop and think, sickness came on the earth because of the sins of Adam and Eve.

> **Before I go any farther, please understand, that because someone is sick, that doesn't mean that they have sinned, it does mean that this body is the last part of fallen man to be delivered. My Soul has been redeemed, my Mind must be renewed daily; I will not have a new Body until the rapture takes place.**

Acts 10:38
How God anointed Jesus of Nazareth with the Holy Ghost and with power: who went about doing good, and healing all that were <u>oppressed of the devil</u>; for God was with him.

The writer of the Book of Acts equates sickness with the oppression of the devil. Ask yourself, does anyone like being sick? So, sickness is oppression. This is one of the hardest lessons for the believer to learn and understand.

They either have someone who is sick or they know someone who is "a good Christian" and they are sick. I've heard people say, "If God doesn't heal them" or "If they don't make it no one will." How easy it is to forget that it's not us in control but God. And He knows all about us, even our future.

Stop and remember what Christ did for us on the Cross. He died to cleanse us from sin. But He also was striped for our healing. It is easier to believe that any sinner that will come to Jesus and ask for forgiveness will receive it because that is why Christ died. But we forget that He died to take away the curse of sin. What is it? Because of Adam's sin, the curse came on the earth and all mankind. When Christ died He delivered us from not just one curse but all, which includes sickness.

As long as the believer doesn't even believe in demons, they can hide themselves in the church and rule over the church through people who are demonized, controlled by demon spirits. We forget that the writing of the Apostle Paul who wrote to the believer and told that there were four classes of demons.

Ephesians 6:12
For we wrestle not against flesh and blood, but against principalities, against powers, against the rulers of the darkness of this world, against spiritual wickedness in high places.

Beware of "Causal spirits/demons."

Demons Can Cause Sickness

One way that Satan and demons seek to hinder the plan and purpose of God is by causing sickness. Unless a Spirit-filled believer knows and stands on the Word of God concerning healing, demons have the power to make them sick.

All through the New Testament, Jesus cast out demonic spirits that had caused blindness, dumbness, epilepsy, leprosy, cancers, arthritis, bone diseases, etc. Let me stop and say that I know that there are physical imbalances that are not the direct work of demons. However, disease is an attack from demons on the human body.

There are many reasons why people don't receive their healing. Some break natural laws, in other words, if you smoke you are asking for lung cancer, and this applies to many other things. Because so many have started to chew tobacco now they are saying that they run the big risk of having month cancer. So when we break the law of nature that God has put in place we are asking for trouble. Another reason is that some people just don't really believe in their heart that healing is for them. Others may have hidden sins, but behind all these reasons is still the devil working to blind the minds, wills, and understanding of people.

I have been asked many times, "Do you believe that there is a demon behind every sickness?" And I have to answer YES! Ultimately everything good comes from above, and we know that sickness is not good, so Satan/Demons must want me sick. The goal of sickness is to kill you and Jesus said in John 10:10, **"The thief cometh not, but for to steal, and to kill, and to destroy: I am come** *that they might have life, and that they might have it more abundantly."* Stop and think about it, if Satan can't stop you from living for the Lord he'll try and kill you to stop you from fulfilling your destiny in the kingdom of God.

> **Jesus came that we can have health: mentally, physically, and spiritually.**

The Battle Is Won, But the War Is Not Over

The reason so many Christians can't get and keep the victory is that they just don't understand the BATTLE TACTICS OF THEIR ENEMY. Just in connection with sickness look at how we act. If we go to the doctor and he tells us that this medicine will taste terrible and will make us feel worse for a while, we then will take the medicine day after day thinking that just any day we'll feel better. If you can trust the words of your doctor how much more should we trust God's Word for our deliverance?

People come for deliverance giving the appearance of wanting whatever God has for them (and for the moment they genuinely do), but then, as they make a start and the Holy Spirit searches their heart and soul, they begin to glimpse and FEEL for themselves, in their emotions and bodies, the true situation and what God see in them. The whole truth is always more than we suspect and as the Holy Spirit reveals to us who and what we really are it is not easy to deal with.

> **The closer to the heart of the problem the Holy Spirit touches, the greater the pressure will be from the powers of darkness to hide and many times will cause the person to altogether withdraw physically, then mentally, and spiritually.**

Is It Possible That We Can Be Our Worst Hindrance?

Of course the answer is YES! Just look at how the world views things. If you are strong-willed and very dominate, they think that is the kind of person they want to work for them. BUT, the Word of God says that when we are weak He is strong.

2 Corinthians 12:10
Therefore I take pleasure in infirmities, in reproaches, in necessities, in persecutions, in distresses for Christ's sake: for when I am weak, then am I strong.

The world looks at what and how we preach and teach and call it foolish, but God looks at it a different way.

1 Corinthians 1:27
But God hath chosen the foolish things of the world to confound the wise; and God hath chosen the weak things of the world to confound the things which are mighty;

> **It's all about "WHO IS IN CONTROL" you or God?**

The more you are in control the less you will yield control to the Lord. I have seen this all around the world, the hardest person to get delivered is the strong-willed person. Almost on the same level is the highly educated. They think they know it all and if it were true they would have already had it or heard of it at least. SATAN blinds their eyes and causes them not to receive what God wants to do for them.

Many dominating people have come for deliverance but very few stay long enough to get any real measure of the blessing that God has for them. WHY? They want to dictate to you how you should minister to them, and secondly, when that fails, they try to go minister to some else's needs (Once again trying to control what's going on). IT'S A SPIRIT that you are dealing with.

If you are to be truly delivered you must come to the place first of all of trusting the person that is doing the Prayer of Deliverance.

The Deliverance Cycle

Satan knows what he did to get a hold on you and each year on the anniversary of your fall he will come to see if you still have your deliverance.

Luke 11:24
When the unclean spirit is gone out of a man, he walketh through dry places, seeking rest; and finding none, he saith, I will return unto my house whence I came out.

Luke 11:25
And when he cometh, he findeth it swept and garnished.

Luke 11:26
Then goeth he, and taketh to him seven other spirits more wicked than himself; and they enter in, and dwell there: and the last state of that man is worse than the first.

THIS IS NOT A ONE TIME TEST, anniversaries are deadly.

Many forget how cunning Satan really is. The Bible tells that demons spirits never give up on you. The question is how good is your deliverance? It's just as good as your walk of faith. You must keep the vessel full and especially on the anniversaries of great struggles.

Luke 11:24
When the unclean spirit is gone out of a man, he walketh through dry places, seeking rest; and finding none, he saith, I will return unto my house whence I came out.

Luke 11:25
And when he cometh, he findeth it swept and garnished.

Luke 11:26
Then goeth he, and taketh to him seven other spirits more wicked than himself; and they enter in, and dwell there: and the last state of that man is worse than the first.

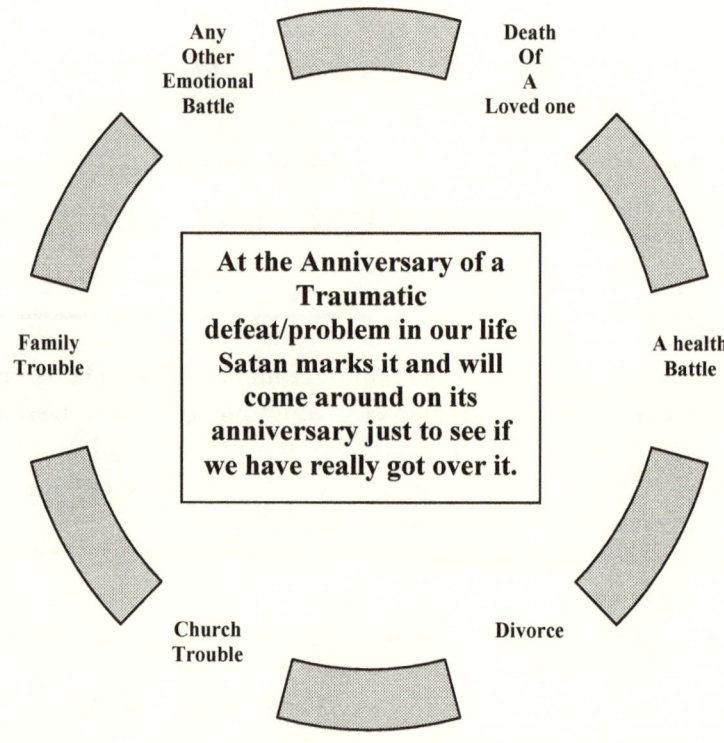

Getting And Keeping The Victory Over The Enemy

Chapter 11

The **"Walk of Faith"** is not just a saying but a life style. ***"For whatsoever is born of God overcometh the world: and this is the victory that overcometh the world, <u>even our faith</u>" (1 John 5:4).*** To get and keep our deliverance it demands a walk of faith.

For most people healing/deliverance is progressive for a variety of reasons and then there are those who see dramatic results instantaneously. There are more, for what ever reason, who receive their deliverance progressively than instantaneously. Some feel great and then because they start to either look for or interpret their SYMPTOMS wrong they lose their faith and Satan tells them it didn't happen.

Stop and think, you can go to a doctor and sometimes the medicine works immediately and then other times the results are not so good. The medicine may not only be very distasteful but may make one's condition feel terrible; however, we usually proceed on the basis that the doctor knows best. Here's my question, if you can trust the doctor in such circumstances, how shouldn't you be able to trust God more?

Remember, it's the results that counts.

Not everyone that comes for prayer to be delivered will receive it nor are they ready to receive it. Stop and think about when you got saved. You had to humble yourself before the Lord and confess your sins, believing that because the Bible said if you would do that, God would forgive your sins.

Romans 10:9-10
That if thou shalt confess with thy mouth the Lord Jesus, and shalt believe in thine heart that God hath raised him from the dead, thou shalt be saved. For with the heart man believeth unto righteousness; and with the mouth confession is made unto salvation.

Everyone that I've led to the Lord, I've used that Scripture with. When they believe what the Word of God says about their condition then they are saved, born-again. They may not look any different, but according to the Word of God now they are a new creature in Christ Jesus.

> **Your very relationship with Christ is based on faith in His Word.**
> *"For by grace are ye saved through faith; and that not of yourselves: it is the gift of God" (Ephesians 2:8).*

If our very salvation depends upon our faith, then our healing/deliverance also depends upon our **faith level.** It is possible for you to believe while you are in the church being prayed for and then when you leave or you feel a pain, lose your faith and think it just didn't happen.

> **I am saved not because of how I feel or look; I am saved because the Word of God says I am when I have confessed my sins from my heart. Then my deliverance is based on the same Word!**

1 John 5:15
And if <u>we know</u> that he hear us, whatsoever we ask, we know that we have the petitions that we desired of him.

How do I know that God has heard my prayer? If I feel the move of the Holy Spirit while I am being prayed for, if I speak in Tongues while I'm being prayed for, if I'm slain in the spirit while I'm being prayed for, don't you think that God has heard? Many times Jesus would look at the people and say, **"Thy faith has made thee whole."** So what are you believing for? More sickness, more problems, more defeat?

> **Why is it that we believe SYMPTOMS more than God's Word?**

A Religious Spirit

The powers of darkness doesn't want the LIGHT to shine in on them. When a man or woman who is anointed by the Spirit confronts the powers of darkness and the Holy Spirit starts to search the inner parts of the person, demons will do whatever they can to stir up a reaction so that they can hide themselves and not be cast out.

The closer to the heart of the problem the ministry touches, the greater the pressure will be from the powers of darkness not to be revealed. Just because you say that you are a Christian and are Spirit-filled, doesn't mean that demon spirits will give up, the word is CAST OUT! That means you must take authority over them, and there are times even with the greatest of Christians that they don't need to be dealing with demon spirits because they are not spiritually nor emotionally ready.

> **Here's food for thought: Domination and being strong-willed in the worldly sense is unclean, and a Christian certainly needs to have those spirits broken off them.** *"Therefore I take pleasure in infirmities, in reproaches, in necessities, in persecutions, in distresses for Christ's sake: for when I am weak, then am I strong" (2 Corinthians 12:10).*

Satan understands a spirit of domination or being strong-willed and he can handle it, but what he can't understand and handle is a humble person, who even though they know that they are weak, can stand in the might and power of the Holy Spirit.

What is a religious spirit? Please understand this! Satan doesn't care about you shouting or speaking in tongues or being slain in the spirit, as long as when you get up all you have done is got a little relief. What I'm saying is don't settle for the shout, being slain, or speaking in tongues, go on past all of that to get FREE! Then you have something to shout about.

Any power of darkness in a person's soul will fight against the Power of the Spirit within a person because

Satan just does not give up. Note what Jesus said *"And from the days of John the Baptist until now the kingdom of heaven suffereth violence, and the violent take it by force" (Matthew 11:12).* Who is the *"violent that take it by force?"* It is the believer. You mean that I've got to be meek in spirit and strong in faith at the same time? YES! The word "violent" which is used here in Strong's # 973, means "**Energetic.**" **Jesus was telling us that it takes courage, unwavering faith, determination, and endurance to enter the kingdom of heaven because of the attacks of the enemy.** The Apostle Paul said *"Finally, my brethren, be strong in the Lord, and in the power of his might." (Ephesians 6:10).*

We understand that when we are weak we are strong, but our strength comes from the LORD! When we fight in our strength we will be defeated, but when we fight in the strength of the Lord we can't help but win.

Understand the "Battle Lines Are Drawn"

Before anyone can get and keep the victory they must have an understanding of the battle lines which are drawn by the Holy Spirit. Failure will cause them to misinterpret their problems, symptoms, and feelings, get discouraged and pull back.

Just as sure as a person wants deliverance Satan will throw in his demons of fear, confusion, and unbelief, very often using those close to us to keep us from receiving our deliverance. But while he is doing that, the Holy Spirit is also waging war on our behalf, and, Thank God, He has promised us victory in the Word of God if we will hold the Faith Level and keep our TRUST in His promises until the victory comes.

> **The greatest battle is not with Satan it's in us, our FAITH LEVEL.**

Satan fights our faith, and if we give in on our faith level then he will get the victory. *"And this is the victory that overcometh the world, EVEN OUT FAITH"* *(1 John 5:4).*

Inside Cleaning Requires Inside Work

One of the hardest things for most people to do is to CHANGE. But to walk in victory will take some changes on our part. Our behaviors and carnal habits must change, we need to cleanse the inner person and yield to the Holy Spirit. Changing the inner person begins by changing our thoughts. Don't forget that the battle ground is in our mind. Our mind plays a large part in our conversion process that we go through when we accept Christ. But to continue the process we must reprogram our minds with the Word of God. Romans 10:17 says *"So then faith cometh by hearing, and hearing by the word of God."*

> **As we plant the Word of God in our minds, it will take root and we will find ourselves saying what God says.**

John 8:31-32
Then said Jesus to those Jews which believed on him, If ye continue in my word, then are ye my disciples indeed; And ye shall know the truth, and the truth shall make you free.

As we start to speak WORDS OF FAITH we will find ourselves saying what God says. We'll start to speak FAITH because the Word will generate positive thoughts and faith thoughts in our minds. Believing you can live a victorious Christian life takes no more effort than believing you cannot. You must chose between God's truth and Satan's lies.

www.ingramcontent.com/pod-product-compliance
Lightning Source LLC
Chambersburg PA
CBHW020915090426
42736CB00008B/648